Emerald Studies in Out-of-School Learning

Parental Engagement and Out-of-School Mathematics Learning

Emerald Studies in Out-of-School Learning

Series Editors: Professor Tim Jay, Loughborough University, and Dr Jo Rose, University of Bristol

Emerald Studies in Out-of-School Learning focuses on the thinking and learning that children engage with outside of school, mainly in primary age groups from 4 to 11 years. Books in the series emphasise the ways in which such out-of-school learning does and does not align with children's classroom learning, and the potential barriers to, and opportunities for, synergy between these two contexts. A key feature of the series is the problematisation of out-of-school learning in terms of its alignment (or otherwise) with classroom learning.

The series will examine some of the complexities of researching out-of-school learning, and the need for new conceptual and methodological approaches and provides a space for work that looks at both informal and formal learning outside of the classroom, and will help to scope and shape this growing discipline.

Parental Engagement and Out-of-School Mathematics Learning: Breaking Out of the Boundaries

BY

TIM JAY

Loughborough University, UK

And

JO ROSE

University of Bristol, UK

emerald
PUBLISHING

United Kingdom – North America – Japan – India – Malaysia – China

Emerald Publishing Limited
Howard House, Wagon Lane, Bingley BD16 1WA, UK

First edition 2023

Reprints and permissions service
Contact: permissions@emeraldinsight.com

British Library Cataloguing in Publication Data
A catalogue record for this book is available from the British Library

ISBN: 978-1-78769-706-5 (Print)
ISBN: 978-1-78769-705-8 (Online)
ISBN: 978-1-78769-707-2 (Epub)

Printed and bound by CPI Group (UK) Ltd, Croydon, CR0 4YY

ISOQAR certified
Management System,
awarded to Emerald
for adherence to
Environmental
standard
ISO 14001:2004.

Certificate Number 1985
ISO 14001

INVESTOR IN PEOPLE

Table of Contents

List of Tables

About the Authors

Tim Jay is Professor of Psychology of Education in the Centre for Mathematical Cognition, Loughborough University. His research focuses on young children's thinking and learning about mathematics. Tim takes an interdisciplinary approach, drawing on theory and methods from psychology, education, computing and design and aims to carry out research that can improve children's experience of mathematics both in and out of school.

Jo Rose is Associate Professor in Social Psychology of Education at the University of Bristol. Her research interests lie in the areas of educational partnerships and collaborative work, particularly in the context of supporting young people from disadvantaged backgrounds. She draws from the disciplines of psychology, sociology and education and particularly enjoys tangling with the myriad of ways that research methods can be combined to understand the complexity of collaboration in the context of education.

Foreword

I am very pleased to write the foreword for this book, not only because Dr Jo Rose and Professor Tim Jay have been friends and colleagues for a number of years, but because this is a book that is timely, important and in particular, very much needed.

Jo, Tim and I share a research interest in parents' engagement in their children's learning; more than that, we are all agreed that this subject is not well enough researched, and frequently misunderstood. We've collaborated before on issues of 'out-of-school learning'; having been through periods of lockdown where almost all learning was 'out of school', the work presented in this book is even more important than it might otherwise have been. Jo and Tim emphasise the importance of relational work – between parents and children and importantly, between school staff and families, as well as between researchers, children, families and school staff. None of us are in the business of supporting learning on our own, even though we often seem to operate as though that were the case.

While there are a good many books about engaging parents in learning, there are few that look at how this can be supported and understood in the area of mathematics; as Jo and Tim point out in this work, maths is often seen as the exception to the rule – what works in other areas (parents supporting learning in the home) is often seen as not applicable to the study of mathematics.

Moreover, Jo and Tim's work over a series of projects has shown that not only is parent engagement in learning often misunderstood (which is a focus of a great deal of my own work), but the very concept of mathematics is also often misconceived. Parents (and school staff) may well maintain that they don't do maths at home with their children, all the while they are counting stairs with young children going up to bed, collecting car number plates to keep older children entertained on long journeys and discussing the intricate matter of just how many points a beloved football team needs to gain to avoid relegation. These are, as Jo and Tim rightly point out, all instances of mathematical thinking, but are rarely considered to be such – rather, maths-at-home is seen as counting change and weighing ingredients because that's what children (and parents) have been told at school.

It's worth pointing out that not everything in this book will be comfortable reading, and I think that's one of the positive things about it. We are enmeshed in educational systems which are frankly iniquitous: children from affluent backgrounds do better in our schooling systems than do their less advantaged contemporaries. If we wish to change that situation – and I do – then we cannot continue to do what we have always done in the past. We cannot, as the clarion cry is so often heard, 'return to normal' after the disruption of the pandemic; 'normal' failed far too many of our children and young people. We need disruption to the system – and Jo and Tim outline how they have gone about such disruption, and the impacts that those changes have had. We need to reconceive how we understand not only parent engagement in learning but also mathematics itself, and research around it.

This book offers insights and suggestions which clearly arise from research grounded in the every day lives (and every day maths) of families and school staff. It suggests ways of moving forward, for parents, teachers and researchers. I particularly recommend it to those in my own context, as schools in Wales move into an era of greater autonomy under the new curriculum. I hope this book will challenge your ideas, support you to reconsider your own practice and thinking in this area, no matter how you relate to children acquiring mathematical understandings.

Janet Goodall
Professor of Education
Swansea University, Department of Education and Childhood Studies

Acknowledgements

Thank you to all those who were part of the work that fed into this book. This includes (but is probably not limited to!): Ulises Xolocotzin and Ben Simmons, for your work as researchers on the respective projects; the schools, children, parents and teachers who participated in the projects; the Leverhulme Trust, the Nuffield Foundation and the ESRC (IAA award) who funded the projects; teachers, parents, colleagues and funders who have discussed the projects' outcomes with us and helped to shape our thinking on what is important, interesting and exciting; Kate Carr-Fanning and Janet Goodall for your supportive feedback on a draft of the book; Emerald Publishers for your enthusiasm for our work; and colleagues, friends and family who have supported us when the writing feels difficult.

Chapter 1

Introduction

This book is about children's out-of-school mathematics learning. Our interest in this area stems from several years of research working with children, parents and teachers, exploring ways in which children think and learn about mathematics out of school, and thinking about ways in which this does and does not align with the kinds of mathematical thinking and learning with which children are expected to engage in the classroom. We are going to start this book by explaining why we think this is an important book to write, and what we hope to achieve by writing it.

Children engage in a wide range of different forms of mathematical thinking and learning out of school that can often be more sophisticated than would be expected of them in the classroom. This will be one of the key themes of the book, as we explore children's play and activity and discuss ways in which we have worked with children and families to find the mathematics in out-of-school lives. There are two important caveats to the claim that children are engaging in sophisticated mathematics outside of the classroom, however. The first is that children are, on the whole, unaware of the mathematics with which they are engaging. This is not to say that children's thinking is disordered or that they are not making good decisions in their contexts, but that children do not always make connections between the thinking that they do outside of school that we might describe as 'mathematical' thinking and their experiences of classroom mathematics. The second caveat is that there are considerable disparities among children's opportunities to engage in activities leading to different forms of mathematical thinking and learning out of school that often align with different social demographic markers. Both of these caveats remind us that out-of-school learning is a challenging phenomenon to study (see also Rose et al., 2022), and that questions about relationships between out-of-school learning and the classroom are complex. We will explore what the research literature can tell us about children's out-of-school thinking and learning later in this chapter and in Chapter 2, and we will begin to share what we have found in our own work in Chapters 3 and 4.

Parents (by which we mean anyone with a caring responsibility for a child, not just biological parents) are very keen to support their children's mathematics learning, but find this difficult to do for a number of reasons. These reasons

Parental Engagement and Out-of-School Mathematics Learning, 1–8
Copyright © 2023 Tim Jay and Jo Rose
Published under exclusive licence by Emerald Publishing Limited
doi:10.1108/978-1-78769-705-820231001

include those to do with the nature of the school mathematics curriculum, difficulties around home-school communication and difficulties connected with their own experience of mathematics and schooling. Much of the time, parents struggle to know what to do for the best. This is important because there is increasing pressure on parents to support children's learning from various sources, and there is a risk of inappropriately blaming parents when children fail to achieve highly in mathematics in schools. As parents are encouraged to do more and more at home to support the learning that children are doing at school, there is also a risk that this reduces the time that parents and children have together for other forms of activity. We will begin to discuss some of the background research literature on parents' role in supporting learning later in Chapter 2, and will share our own research with parents in Chapter 4.

Important opportunities for children to engage with mathematical thinking and learning can sometimes be lost due to ways in which parental involvement is co-opted by schools and related organisations. In acting in the service of schools and schooling, parents can give up their position as the main educator of their children and the associated sense of their own expertise in supporting their children's learning. One of the main outcomes of the research projects that we report in this book has been a way of working with parents that disrupts this kind of parent–school relationship. We have supported parents to 'find the maths' in everyday life and activity and to explore ways of sharing their mathematical thinking with their children. In doing this, parents we have worked with have reconsidered their relationship with mathematics, and the ways in which they support their children's learning, finding for themselves more positive ways to engage with mathematics than they previously had access to. We have then also worked with teachers to encourage this same kind of thinking, and this same kind of relationship, with parents of children in their schools.

The projects that we draw on in this book have led us to explore a number of related issues around children's out-of-school mathematics learning, including, for example: the barriers to children's understanding of connections between out-of-school and classroom mathematics learning; the ways in which school practices limit children's (and parents') engagement with, and reflection on, out-of-school learning and the ethics of intervention studies that challenge education policy. Through the course of the research, we have reflected on the several ways in which we have questioned traditional conceptions and practices in education and educational research in trying to achieve our aims. With this book, we will share these reflections and use our research projects as case studies to make the argument that there is a need for a new approach to educational research that subverts and disrupts traditional models and approaches.

Why Mathematics?

We have chosen to focus on *mathematics* learning in our work, rather than learning of other curriculum subjects or other areas of interest, for a number of connected reasons. One of the authors of this book (Tim) was a secondary school mathematics teacher for a time, and this experience gave him an interest in trying to understand better some of the specific things about mathematics that made it a difficult subject for some children.

A second reason is that mathematics qualifications are used as a way to manage access to further study and other opportunities. At the time of writing, there was discussion within government about the possibility of only allowing undergraduate students to take out a student loan to support their studies if they had a GCSE grade of 4 (approximately equivalent to the previous grade C) or higher in both English and Mathematics (https://www.timeshighereducation.com/news/english-universities-await-clarity-onimpact-ofgcse-entry-bar). Improvement in mathematics learning is a high priority for teachers and parents, and many feel some pressure to find better ways to support children.

A third reason for the focus on mathematics is that we know that parents have particular concerns about supporting learning in this area, relative to other areas of the curriculum. We wanted to learn more about the source of such concerns, and to consider what might be done to alleviate them.

What Counts as Out-of-School?

At this point in the introduction, we need to deal with the questions of 'what counts?' as out-of-school mathematics learning. The term 'out-of-school' is problematic, as it defines a phenomenon in the negative. This negative definition first of all makes out-of-school learning difficult to pin down. The first thing we might think of is learning that happens outside of school *space* – that is outside of school buildings, or school grounds. However, this would mean that the term 'out-of-school learning' would include learning that happens during school trips (to the museum, for example), which is not really what we are thinking about. It turns out that out-of-school *space* is a somewhat fuzzy boundary that doesn't clearly separate one set of activities from another. A second way to deal with 'out-of-school' is to think about out-of-school *time* – which would refer to learning that happens outside of normal school hours, around nine in the morning until three in the afternoon. Again, this is a fuzzy kind of boundary when we consider activities like homework clubs, held outside of normal school time, often after school has finished for the day, to allow children to complete homework set by their teachers. Homework clubs seem very much to be more aligned with school than out-of-school learning, and so the 'out-of-school *time*' label doesn't quite work for us either. A third way to think about 'out-of-school' would be to use it to refer to types of *activity* that are not typically found in school. However, this is perhaps even more fuzzy than the previous two options! While homework, set by a teacher to be completed by children at home, would not count as an out-of-school activity, would we count piano practice as a school activity or an out-of-school activity? How about a child researching the solar system because of an interest in space? How would we determine whether the child's activity was sufficiently different to what they might normally be expected in a classroom to count as 'out-of-school'? So 'out-of-school *activity*' does not work for us either.

We have to decide to be pragmatic about this definition and accept the fact that it may not be possible to create a definition that clearly separates out-of-school learning from the classroom. Instead, we have opted for an inclusive 'we know it when we see it' approach.

Introduction of Key Themes

Throughout the book, we aim to question ways in which out-of-school learning does and does not align with classroom mathematics learning. There is a sense in which we will be questioning the idealistic and reductionist vision that many stakeholders (including representatives of governments, schools and parents) have, where out-of-school activity functions mainly as a means to raise children's school attainment. While we will go into the details of support and evidence for this vision, together with reasons why it may be misconceived, later on in the book, we introduce here some of the main issues and themes that we will be returning to regularly.

Parental Involvement and Parental Engagement

There is universal agreement among researchers and practitioners that parents and families have a tremendous effect on children's development and learning. Once children start formal education, some of the responsibility for children's learning is taken on by teachers, but parents remain a hugely significant influence on children's outcomes. Several reviews show that parental involvement in children's learning lives has a positive influence on academic (Desforges & Abouchaar, 2003) and affective (Fan & Williams, 2009) outcomes. In fact, Desforges and Abouchaar assert that, 'in the primary age range the impact caused by different levels of parental involvement is much bigger than differences associated with variations in the quality of schools' (p. 4.). The difficulty though, in making use of this information, is the fact that parental involvement is not a simple construct, but made up of a variety of activities and attitudes. Some of these activities and attitudes include aspects of home life, including the quantity and quality of conversation with children (McNeal, 2001; Sui-Chu & Williams, 1996), the provision of a suitable home learning environment (Melhuish et al., 2008), parents' aspirations and expectations for their children (Garg et al., 2002; Ma, 2001; Mau, 1997) and parents' formal teaching of their children (Skwarchuk et al., 2014) – especially in early reading and number. Parental support of extra-curricular activities (including sports, music, arts and other activities) has also been shown to correlate strongly with children's affective and academic outcomes (Bradley & Conway, 2016; Chanfreau et al., 2016). And then there are the positive effects of parental involvement in children's school lives (Fan & Williams, 2009; Goodall & Montgomery, 2014).

So parental involvement in children's learning potentially comprises several areas of activity, each one with its own contribution to children's learning. This makes it difficult to say with any certainty which aspects of activity have what effects on children's outcomes – be they academic, social or otherwise. A second complicating factor is that as well as varying in quantity, all of these activities vary in *quality* – in other words how parents and families carry them out. There is a good example of this in Fan and William (2009); they found that contact between parents and school regarding benign issues was positively associated with motivation outcomes, whereas contact between parents and school regarding children's difficulties was negatively associated with these outcomes. Another area where the quality of activity appears to be very important is homework. While some reports suggest that parental help and support in completion of homework is positively associated with attainment (Fan et al., 2017), others, including a meta-analysis reported by Patall et al. (2008) suggest that parental involvement in homework at this age may be negatively associated with attainment in some cases. Patall et al. found that parental involvement with reading homework was associated with positive outcomes, while involvement with mathematics outcomes was associated with negative outcomes. They suggest that this may be because parents focus more on a monitoring role with respect to mathematics homework, in comparison to sharing activities in reading.

For now, suffice it to say that the ways in which parents are involved in, or choose to support, children's learning, have large effects on children's learning, and their academic and effective outcomes. The only problem, and one that we will return to, is that it is very difficult to know what kinds of parental involvement have what effects.

Education Policy

Perhaps driven by some of the research referred to above, some governments have written parental involvement into legislation. For example, the Scottish Schools (Parental Involvement) Act (2006) requires local authorities to have a strategy in place to improve parental involvement in education in three ways; encouraging learning at home, improving home–school partnership and increasing parental representation in school governance. Similarly, the US No Child Left Behind Act (2001) sets out expectations of schools and local authorities in order to improve home–school relationships and increase parental involvement in children's learning. While not always enacted in law, English schools often have parental involvement policies, and advice and guidance is available from the Department of Education (Desforges & Abouchaar, 2003; Goodall & Voorhaus, 2011), NGOs (e.g. Education Endowment Foundation[1]) and charities (e.g. National Numeracy[2]).

While no doubt driven by good intentions, government and school policies to increase the quantity and/or quality of parental involvement in children's education and learning have the potential for unintended negative consequences. The research briefly summarised above tells us that more parental involvement tends to lead to better outcomes for children; so why should we be concerned about policy that aims for more parental involvement? There are actually a few reasons why policy efforts to increase or improve parental involvement could be detrimental. Firstly, studies that have provided the best evidence of positive effects of parental involvement have tended to be correlational; studies with the potential to demonstrate cause, or that aim to demonstrate the effectiveness of parental involvement interventions in improving children's learning, have been less successful in demonstrating positive effects. Secondly, as discussed previously, the research to date does not give us 'one size fits all' guidance for what parents should be doing. There is definitely a sense, though, that more is not always better, and that the quality of parental involvement is likely to be at least as important as the quantity. Thirdly, a major risk of policy initiatives to raise levels of parental involvement in children's learning is that it can create a deficit model of parental behaviour; this in turn can lead parents, and those working with parents, to have more negative views of parents' abilities and behaviours, leading to reduced levels of involvement in children's education and learning. We will explore each of these issues a little further here.

No 'One Size Fits All'

Crozier warns against one-size-fits-all interventions for supporting parental engagement; not all parents are the same, have the same needs, face the same barriers or share the same conceptualisation of parental engagement (Crozier, 1999, 2001). This principle connects with a key issue for us in our work researching and encouraging parental engagement in mathematics learning; that of avoiding a deficit model approach in our interactions with and thinking about parents. In fact, one of the motivations for us in pursuing this line of research is the number of times that an educational professional has told us something like, 'Our parents are rubbish'. While obviously somewhat disappointing to hear, we interpret these kinds of statement as a problem to be addressed, rather than an objective comment on the 'quality' of parents of children at a school. These statements tell us that teachers in some schools recognise that there are problems of communication and of expectations that need to be solved before teachers and parents feel that they are working together in a positive and constructive way to support children's learning.

One step that may be required for teachers and parents to work together in a constructive way is some reframing of relative responsibilities for difficulties. 'Hard to reach' is a phrase that many teachers use to describe groups of parents that are not regularly engaged in school activity and who teachers suspect may not be supporting children's learning at home as well as they might. Crozier and Davies (2007) provide some useful insight here when they suggest that rather than considering *parents* as being hard for *schools and teachers* to reach, that we can instead usefully consider schools and teachers as being hard for parents to reach. Crozier and Davies found that parents that they worked with in their study had very positive attitudes towards their children's education and learning, and were not 'obstructive' or 'difficult'. Rather, the structures and actions of schools and teachers frequently inhibited parental engagement among some groups of parents.

For us, there are clear links between some other sections of this chapter, and a sense that a one-size-fits-all approach to parental engagement is not an effective way to improve learning. This may, for example, help to explain why many trials of interventions intended to improve parental engagement have not been successful. Where interventions are implemented at scale, without sufficient adaptation to the particular needs and context of schools and parent populations, they are unlikely to be successful. Similarly, if teachers responsible for implementing interventions as part of a trial are not fully committed to working closely with parents and families to adapt a programme to their particular needs and context, then again the trial is unlikely to show improved learning.

Returning to that 'Our parents are rubbish' statement, we suggest that some teachers may at times have a model of the 'ideal' parent that parents of children in their school are not perceived to live up to. This starting point means that such teachers can think about what might help parents support their children's learning in a certain way, and often this involves trying to teach parents new knowledge and skills that they are perceived to lack. A big part of our work has been about empowering parents to use their existing knowledge and skills and to see how parents negotiate their own approaches to parental engagement when encouraged to do so.

Outlines of Chapters

Chapter 2 builds on this introduction by diving into the detail of relevant literature in this field. We explore previous research on parental engagement with schools and learning in general, before looking specifically at engagement with mathematics learning in particular. We also explore research on cultural differences in out-of-school mathematics thinking and learning, and consider previous efforts to develop interventions to improve parental engagement. Finally, we outline the gaps in the literature that we have attempted to address with our own work.

Chapters 3 and 4 describe two of the projects that have formed the foundations of our work in this area. Chapter 3 focuses on 'Children's economic activity and mathematics learning'. This project, funded by the Leverhulme Trust, allowed us to investigate children's economic activity outside of school as a locus for mathematical thinking and learning. We were interested to see how the mathematical thinking and learning that children engaged in as part of this self-directed and self-motivated activity did or did not align with the mathematical thinking and learning that children experience in their classrooms. Chapter 4 focuses on 'The Everyday Maths project', in which we worked with groups of parents to explore barriers to effective engagement with children's mathematics learning, and develop activities and resources to empower parents to work around these barriers and to support their children's mathematics learning effectively.

In Chapters 5–9 we further develop some themes through our thinking and reflections on our research. In Chapter 5, 'The politics of purpose,' we look at ways in which different agencies and stakeholders involved in children's education often have different purposes in mind. We explore how this can give rise to problematic situations and how these might be resolved. Chapter 6, 'Methods of engagement', looks at the importance of good relationships in fostering effective parental engagement in learning. We consider approaches we have taken to developing positive relationships between parents, teachers and researchers, and reflect on what we have learnt through our research. In Chapter 7, we consider 'The "what" and the "how" of our projects: participants' expectations about our research' and discuss how we have managed the introduction of quite novel, and therefore sometimes uncomfortable, approaches for teachers and parents to think about supporting children's learning. In Chapter 8, we broaden out these discussions in 'Exploring uncertain territory'. Here we discuss how we, as the research team, managed working on projects where we needed to let go of some of the control of exactly where studies went and what we might find. In Chapter 9, 'The ethics of disruption', we reflect on ways in which we have set out to change relationships and disrupt usual practices in the course of our research. We consider ways in which this has presented risks and how we have justified and ameliorated such risks in our work.

In Chapter 10, we describe some of the challenges of translating research to practice in this field. We discuss some of our work with teachers and reflect on some of the challenges of scaling up research in parental engagement in mathematics learning. And finally, in Chapter 11, we share some concluding reflections on the research presented in this book and discuss some ways in which we hope that this research might inform future research and practice in education.

Chapter 2

Previous Research on Out-of-School Mathematics Learning and Parental Engagement

In this chapter we build on Chapter 1 and survey the previous research that has most strongly influenced our thinking in carrying out the projects that we discuss in this book. This chapter is divided into three main sections. First, we focus on what we know about children's mathematics learning out of school. We discuss what previous research tells us about how children's out-of-school mathematics learning might compare with their mathematics learning that takes place in classrooms, and about how children's out-of-school mathematics learning might vary among groups of children including ways that connect with culture and background. Second, we focus on what previous research has told us about parents' role in supporting learning in general, and mathematics learning in particular. And finally, we look at what previous research tells us about schools' efforts to improve parental engagement with children's learning, through programmes and interventions. These surveys of what previous research can tell us in these three areas will lead towards some discussion of where we identified some key gaps and open questions that we addressed in our own research.

Children's Out-of-School Mathematics Learning

Research on mathematics in the home has shown us that families often draw on distinctive funds of knowledge that include skills and strategies that can be qualitatively different to the mathematical knowledge that children are taught in school (Baker & Street, 2004; González et al., 2006). For example, Baker et al. (2003) report an account of a child who has learnt to count three to a finger when using her fingers to count a set of objects. In the report, this was revealed to be a family practice. The child's parents counted in this way because they said that it was more useful than counting one to a finger; counting three to a finger allowed them to count a set of up to 30 objects while counting one to a finger only allows for 10. Baker, Street and Tomlin go on to discuss ways in which these kinds of

Parental Engagement and Out-of-School Mathematics Learning, 9–17
Copyright © 2023 Tim Jay and Jo Rose
Published under exclusive licence by Emerald Publishing Limited
doi:10.1108/978-1-78769-705-820231002

home and family practices then integrate or otherwise with practices learnt in the classroom at school.

Families often engage in problem-solving which requires considerable mathematical knowledge and practice (Goldman & Booker, 2009). Goldman and Booker report case studies of three different families engaging in problem-solving around their day-to-day activities: preparing for prom; attending a baseball game and organising themselves to get to school on time in the morning. These case studies provide some detail of the mathematical thinking and learning involved in everyday family activity – for example, in the 'preparing for prom' case study, there are discussions of how much budget to allow, how to prioritise different wants and needs and how to save on some aspects to allow more money for others. However, an important finding for Goldman and Booker across the three case studies was that families did not think of this kind of activity as 'mathematical'. They write, 'They [the families] viewed their attentions and engagements as dealing with life; their definitions of the situations were context and activity based, not epistemological in nature' (p. 384), and, '... the parents in our study did not typically think of their lives as mathematically rich or complex because they had not really considered the mathematics they practiced in their daily problem posing and problem solving beyond the more obvious basic calculations' (p. 384). A good deal of the work that we report in this book stems from our own noticing of this phenomenon – that families engage in a good deal of mathematical thinking and learning in their everyday lives, but often do not recognise or explicitly talk about such activity as mathematical. This has in turn led us to ask ourselves whether there might be opportunities to draw families' attention to such activity as 'mathematical' and find ways to draw on mathematical activity in everyday life more explicitly as a resource for learning.

Research Connecting Out-of-School With Classroom Mathematics Learning

Attempts to connect home and school mathematics demonstrate that day-to-day household situations offer a context that is rich in opportunities for children to learn and apply different forms of mathematics (Winter et al., 2004). Mathematics can often appear to be a subject that exists in a purely abstract state, having little relation to culture. However, research shows that mathematical thinking and learning can have much more to do with learners' backgrounds and culture than we might intuitively think.

A classic example of out-of-school mathematics learning is provided by Carraher et al. (1985). In this study, the researchers worked with child street vendors in Recife, Brazil, and found that these children's ability to solve arithmetic problems in the context of their work far outstripped their ability to solve equivalent problems in a more formal context. This study demonstrated the way in which informal out-of-school thinking and learning in mathematics does not necessarily transfer to formal, classroom, contexts. Despite participants' facility with mathematical operations in ways that were directly relevant to their lives and work, it was not immediately possible for them to transfer this understanding and apply it in an alternative context. Of course, the study raises as many questions as it answers. We do not know from Carraher et al., for example, how much instruction or support would have enabled their participants to have answered problems in a more formal context correctly – although this was not possible immediately, it may be that their informal understandings would have made it possible for them to demonstrate understanding in formal contexts relatively quickly with some support.

Gonzalez et al. (2006) use the phrase 'funds of knowledge' to describe the socially and culturally based knowledge and skills that learners bring with them to any learning context. These researchers advocate for teaching innovations that bring children's funds of knowledge into the classroom, with a view to making the classroom experience richer and more meaningful for those children (Moll et al., 1992). In the United Kingdom, the Home-School Knowledge Exchange project (Hughes & Pollard, 2006) built on the work of Moll and others to use the funds of knowledge concept to improve teaching and parental engagement in primary schools and in the transition from primary to secondary school. The research team highlighted some of the challenges involved in putting the theory into practice, including finding ways to work with a diversity of family backgrounds and experience, and supporting teachers to value funds of knowledge of families with very different culture and backgrounds to themselves.

More recent research has looked at mathematics and other STEM (science, technology, engineering and mathematics) learning activity that happens outside of school, and how this out-of-school learning does and does not align with children's classroom learning experience (e.g. Bevan et al., 2013). A key observation in much of this research has been than children from more deprived backgrounds and those belonging to minority ethnic groups engage with out-of-school learning opportunities that are much less likely to align with their classroom learning experiences than other children. This is something that we have been keen to address in our research, in two main ways. Firstly, we aimed in our interactions with families to recognise and value the ways that families engage in mathematical talk and activity, regardless of how this talk and activity resembled or did not resemble the mathematical talk and activity that usually takes place in classrooms. Secondly, we aimed in our interactions with teachers to draw teachers' awareness towards ways of talking and thinking about mathematics that do not necessarily align with their expectations of what counts as good classroom mathematics learning. We have been interested just to notice what happens when we draw attention to, and valorise, the mathematical talk and activity that occurs in families around everyday life, regardless of background or culture, or the extent to which family mathematical talk and activity resembles the kinds of activity we might expect to see in a mathematics classroom.

Parents' Role Supporting Children's Mathematics Learning

There is good evidence to show that children's experience of mathematics outside of the classroom is an important contributor to their learning. This is the case right from children's earliest years. For example, Levine et al. (2010) observed mothers and their 14-to 30-month-old children in naturalistic contexts during 5 90-minute sessions spaced 4 months apart. They looked at the quantity of number words from 1 to 10 spoken by mothers, as well as their use of words including 'count', 'how many' and 'number' (i.e. number elicitations). Over the 5 sessions, they saw a range from a total of 4 to 257 number words and from 0 to 30 uses of parent elicitation of child number talk. So extrapolating from these data, we can assume that there is huge variation in the amount of number talk that children are exposed to at home. Levine et al. also took a measure of children's knowledge of cardinal number at the end of the data collection period at 30 months of age and found that volume of number talk was strongly correlated with number knowledge.

In a similar study, Susperreguy and Davis-Kean (2016) recorded 4 hours of talk at meal-times with children aged 4–5 years old. Examples of maths talk ranged from 4 to 195 instances. Susperreguy and Davis-Kean (2016) found that the proportion of mothers' talk that included mathematics predicted children's mathematical ability 1 year later. Levine et al. (2010) and Susperreguy and Davis-Kean (2016) are important in informing thinking in this field, as in both studies, parents were not aware that the researchers' focus was on number and mathematics. Both studies show that everyday talk and play around family activity is important for children's learning, and that this talk and play does not need to be formal or guided to be effective in supporting children's learning, especially while children are young and in the early stages of number learning.

The examples above of research on parents' and children's spontaneous number talk provide useful context for this discussion, but it is important to note that this kind of spontaneous talk may be quite different to interactions that are actually intended by the parent to contribute to children's learning. And in fact, the research shows that when parental engagement is more formal and guided, then outcomes for children tend to be more mixed. An example of this can be found in research on parental involvement in children's homework. Homework is often set by schools for children to do at home, as a way to increase the amount of time that children spend on thinking and learning, with a view to increasing levels of attainment. Homework is also sometimes seen by schools as a locus for thinking about and encouraging parental involvement in learning. Patall et al. (2008) reviewed the available literature on the effects of parental involvement with homework on children's attainment. Across the studies included in their meta-analysis, they found only very small, marginally significant, effects of parental involvement on children's outcomes. In their analyses of potential moderator variables, they found that the type of parental involvement, and the subject being studied appeared to affect the relationship between volume of involvement and effect on attainment. For the type of parental involvement, they found that outcomes for children were better when parental involvement comprised monitoring of homework completion and keeping children on task when completing homework, and outcomes were worse when parents gave feedback on children's work or when they otherwise attempted to tutor children in completion of work. With respect to the subject being studied, outcomes for children were better when parents were involved with homework in verbal and language subjects, and worse when the homework was on mathematics. In fact, across the studies included in the meta-analysis the correlation between parental involvement in mathematics homework and children's outcomes was negative, meaning that the more that parents were involved, the less children learnt.

It is not fully clear why children's mathematics learning may be more difficult to engage with for parents than other subjects. However, there are some clues in the literature. For example, we know that parents sometimes experience mathematics anxiety in a way that they do not experience when working in other areas of the curriculum with their children (Gunderson et al., 2012). Further to this, Maloney et al. (2015) have found that when parents are more anxious about mathematics, their children learn significantly less over the course of a school year and have more anxiety about mathematics themselves by the end of the school year – but only if parents report providing frequent help with mathematics homework. Peters et al. (2008) add to this with their finding that parents' main reasons for lacking confidence in supporting children's learning were changing teaching methods and a lack of understanding of the child's work; these issues are often particularly challenging in mathematics. In our own research (Jay et al., 2018), we have heard similar reports from parents – that even where parents have a good understanding of the mathematics involved, they often struggle with the methods being used as these are unfamiliar to them.

Parental Influences on Children's Learning at School

Over the last 30 years, there have been several studies showing a correlation between parental engagement in children's education and various outcomes for children. Early studies grew out of the work of psychologists including Bronfenbrenner (1986), who developed an ecological model of children's development that highlighted the importance of the family in determining outcomes for children. The work of researchers including Chavkin (1993) and Epstein (1983, 1991) built a foundation of evidence connecting school and teacher practices with parental engagement leading to improvements in children's academic progress. These studies paved the way for some large-scale correlational studies showing associations between various forms of parental involvement in children's education and children's attainment on assessments at primary and secondary school levels (e.g. Flouri & Buchanan, 2004; Melhuish et al., 2008). These warrant some closer attention as they have been important references for much of the research carried out on parental engagement since.

Flouri and Buchanan (2004) drew on a large sample from the National Child Development Survey (NCDS). This study was interesting because it was able to explore the effects of mothers' and fathers' involvement at age seven independently of one another and was also able to control for a relatively large number of potential confounds, including children's gender, birthweight and cognitive, emotional and behavioural factors, parental socioeconomic status and education, and family structure, size and mobility. Mothers' and fathers' involvement at age

7 were tested as predictors of academic outcomes at age 20. On the other hand, this study was limited by the relatively coarse-grained measures of parental involvement contained in the NCDS. In NCDS there were four 3-point scales for father involvement and three 3-point scales for mother involvement at age 7. The items on father involvement were 'outings with father', 'father manages the child', 'father reads to child' and 'father is interested in child's education'.

The items on mother involvement were 'outings with mother', 'mother reads to child' and 'mother is interested in child's education'; each item was a 3-point Likert scale. In this study, control variables accounted for 52% of the variance in academic outcomes at age 20. Father involvement accounted for an additional 0.4% of the variance, and mother involvement accounted for an additional 0.5%. Although these contributions to the regression model with highly statistically significant, the effect sizes were clearly very small.

Melhuish et al. (2008) collected data from more than 2000 families. This included a semi-structured interview with a parent at age 3 and a set of academic outcomes, focussing on reading and mathematics, at age 7. Data from the interviews at age 3 were used to derive a measure of the Home Learning Environment (HLE). This measure of parental involvement was more fine-grained than that used in Flouri and Buchanan (2004), but still only drew on seven activities – each assessed on a 7-point scale. In this study the HLE measure accounted for 10% of the variance in reading and 6% of the variance in mathematics attainment at age 7 – although this study did not control for as many potential confounds as did Flouri and Buchanan (2004).

Both Flouri and Buchanan (2004) and Melhuish et al. (2008) provide evidence that parental involvement is a highly significant factor in children's academic attainment. However, both also show that involvement does not necessarily have a large effect on attainment, after other correlated variables, including socio-economic status, parental education and family stability, have been taken into account. A further complicating factor, though, is that analysis of these two studies shows that it is very difficult to determine the effect of involvement on attainment with any accuracy. Although both studies collected large volumes of longitudinal data, and took account of a number of potential confounds, they reveal some important methodological challenges in this area of work. Perhaps the most important of these challenges is the difficulty in creating a measure or measures of parental involvement. Flouri and Buchanan (2004) used a measure that assessed the extent to which parents read with their child, went on outings with their child and took an interest in their child's education. Melhuish et al. (2008) used a measure that assessed the frequency that a child: was read to; went to the library; played with numbers; did painting and drawing; was taught letters; was taught numbers or was taught songs/poems/rhymes, with a parent. While both of these measures clearly capture some of the activity that parents engage in that supports children's learning, many such activities will be missing. Also, both measures are unable to capture anything about the quality of such activity or interaction – both focus exclusively on the quantity or frequency of activity. In large-scale studies like this the focus on quantity over quality is perhaps unavoidable, but this still raises some questions about how we should interpret or react to their findings. We suggest that these large-scale studies are valuable in focussing our attention on parental involvement as an area of study and as a potential site of intervention for improving outcomes for children, but also that on their own they do not provide any guidance about what parents should do for their children. Alongside these kinds of studies, we need to understand more about what constitutes quality in parental involvement in children's learning.

Parental Involvement in Schooling and Parental Engagement in Learning

Goodall and Montgomery (2014) propose a model for thinking about different ways that parents can participate in children education. They described a continuum, from 'parental involvement' at one end, to 'parental engagement' at the other. Parental involvement is described as involvement in school life and includes attendance at parents' evenings and school events, participation in parent–teacher association meetings and events and support for school-led learning interventions such as completion of homework tasks. Parental engagement, on the other hand, involves parent-led activity with a focus on real engagement with children's learning. Goodall and Montgomery suggest that activity at all points on the continuum has potential for positive outcomes, but that there is often a relative lack of parental engagement with children's learning compared with efforts made towards parental involvement with schools and schooling.

Government Policies on Parental Engagement With Children's Learning

Before moving on to research that addresses the issue of quality in parental involvement, we raise the fact that government policy within the United Kingdom and internationally has advised and sometimes mandated school promotion and support for parental involvement. In England, guidance and research reports describe the benefits of parental involvement. For example, a document published by the Department for Children, Schools, and Families (2008) advocates for increased parental involvement to improve children's attainment, and parental involvement was cited in the development of 'free schools' policy in a white paper published by the Department for Education in 2010. In Scotland, the Scottish Schools [Parental Involvement] Act (2006) makes it the duty of local education authorities to 'promote the involvement of the parents of a pupil in attendance at a public school in the authority's area in the education provided by the school – (a) to that pupil, and (b) to its pupils generally' and mandates that each education authority publish its own strategy for parental involvement.

In 2014, the US Department for Education published a framework for parental and community engagement (see also Mapp & Kuttner, 2013). Similarly, the Australian government has a policy to increase parental involvement in education, as does the Ontario Ministry for Education (2010). However, although there are pushes to develop such work, there is often a lack of guidance regarding how to develop an effective approach.

Why Do Interventions to Improve Parental Engagement in Mathematics Learning Often Fail?

The rationale for the inclusion of parental engagement in education policy tends to be that large-scale correlational research (such as that discussed above) suggests a connection between higher levels of parental engagement and higher levels of pupil attainment in schools. Policymakers can often assume that because of this, it should be relatively straightforward to increase pupil attainment by encouraging more parental engagement with children's learning through teachers' actions. However, while there is indeed evidence that suggests that parental involvement can have positive effects on children's achievement and attitudes, recent systematic reviews have found only limited evidence that parental involvement interventions result in improved educational outcomes. This is important and warrants more focus in research, practice and policymaking. It is clearly not straightforward to increase levels of parental engagement with the expectation that this will lead to easy gains in pupil outcomes. For example, Desforges and Abouchaar (2003) carried out a review of the available literature and concluded that evidence for parental involvement interventions was too weak to come to any firm conclusions about their efficacy. Similarly, Gorard and Huat See (2013) reviewed 756 evaluations of parental involvement (of these, only 68 met criteria for design quality) and found no evidence for improvement in educational outcomes:

> Overall, we found no evidence that primary-age interventions to enhance parental involvement are generally effective in increasing children's attainment. In fact, the better studies suggest the interventions can be harmful. (p. 7)

Some conflicting evidence is provided by Jeynes (2012) in the form of a meta-analysis of 51 evaluations of the effect of parental involvement programs on pupil attainment. Jeynes found an average effect size of 0.3 overall, suggesting a small but significant effect, with programmes focussing on shared reading and on partnership between parents and teachers having the largest effects. It is not clear why the conclusions of Gorard and Huat See (2013) differ so dramatically from those of Jeynes (2012). However, Gorard and Huat See had stricter criteria for inclusion in their review, and Jeynes included a number of studies with small sample sizes. Both Gorard and Huat See and Jeynes make a case for further research that addresses the reasons why parental involvement programs succeed or fail in raising student achievement. Given the current lack of understanding of what might constitute a successful parental engagement intervention, this appears to be an important step.

There is little discussion in the literature specifically regarding the reasons why parental involvement interventions may fail. One reason may be that too few programmes involve a comprehensive approach (Redding et al., 2004). Redding et al. (2004) argue that, if it is to be successful, a parental involvement programme must be built on a foundation of trust and respect and must connect parental involvement strategies with students' learning objectives. Some recent review articles suggest some further potential candidates. Hornby and Lafaele (2011) reviewed the literature on parental involvement and posited several potential barriers to parents becoming involved in their children's education. Many are based on the fact that parents' and teachers' aims around parental involvement, while similar in some ways, differ in important respects. For example, Hornby and Lafaele point to research showing that teachers' aims are often to improve the school or wider society, whereas parents' aims often relate to their individual child's well-being or performance relative to the child's peers. Implicit in Hornby and Lafaele's review is the idea that some difficulties around parental involvement stem from parents' and teachers' understanding that parental involvement is to be engaged with in the service of school- and government-defined measures of attainment. Based on this and on related work (e.g. Jay et al., 2017; Peters et al., 2008) that describes parents' own negative experiences of schooling, we contend that many parents experience a distance from and a lack of ownership of the formal school curriculum that contributes to the difficulties they experience in supporting their children's school learning.

Summary and Introduction to Next Chapters

Most research on parental engagement in children's mathematics learning has been 'school-centred' rather than child- or (especially) parent-centred. From Goodall and Montgomery's (2014) framework we would see this as involvement rather than engagement, with parents being asked to support the work of the school (including the school's approach to mathematics teaching) rather than engage meaningfully with their individual child's education and learning. This is a wasted opportunity, as parents are often the only people really in a position to give children personalised learning support – including making connections between areas of learning and a children's interests and experience. A major aim of the work we describe in this book is about regressing the balance and exploring ways to empower parents to genuinely engage with their children's mathematical thinking and learning.

The following two chapters describe two projects that we carried out in order to learn more about children's out-of-school mathematics activity and to try to develop ways to draw more explicitly on this activity as a source for learning. In the first, we focus more on working directly with children – using a range of research methods to learn more about children's out-of-school activity and the mathematical thinking and learning involved. In the second, we focus more on working with parents – exploring family activity as a resource for mathematics learning and working with parents to think about how to use such activity as a resource to support children's learning out of school. We then look across the two projects to explore some issues in depth. These include looking at the importance of building relationships, the importance of challenging unhelpful conceptions of education and learning, and the importance of willingness to disrupt existing practices, all of which are necessary from our point of view to do this research well and to promote successful parental engagement with children's mathematics learning effectively.

Chapter 3

The Economic Activity and Mathematics Learning Project

Introduction

This project took place between 2011 and 2013 in Bristol, in the United Kingdom. The main aim of the project was to explore the mathematical thinking and learning that children experience out of school. This was motivated by a combination of factors. On the one hand, we drew on research in education telling us that there is limited understanding of the kinds of experience that children are drawing on in the mathematics classroom, or of how mathematics teachers can best make use of children's out-of-school experience in their teaching. On the other hand, we drew on research in economic psychology which told us there was useful work to be done in research children's economic activity and learning from their own point of view. The literature on out-of-school mathematics learning has been thoroughly covered in Chapter 2, but research on children's economic activity warrants some attention here.

Children's Economic Activity From Their Own Point of View

Children as young as six years old understand economic concepts such as supply and demand (Leiser & Beth Halachmi, 2006), and there is a fairly well-established literature showing how children come to develop other conceptions of how the adult financial world works (Berti et al., 1988). However, more recent research has focussed on ways in which children construct their own understandings of economic concepts, that help to make sense of their own activity. A key text in this area is Webley and Lea's (1993) description of the 'marble economy' that they observed in school playgrounds in England. For example, children developed their own rules about the value of different marbles that did not correspond to the price of such marbles in shops but connected closely with scarcity and availability in the playground – children were able to explain why it was that different kinds of marbles had different values. Further, these researchers observed the phenomenon of marble 'capitalists' coming to arrangements with 'workers' (these are the researchers' labels, not the children's). The capitalists had large supplies of marbles, and the workers were expert marbles players. The researchers

Parental Engagement and Out-of-School Mathematics Learning, 19–29
Copyright © 2023 Tim Jay and Jo Rose
Published under exclusive licence by Emerald Publishing Limited
doi:10.1108/978-1-78769-705-820231003

documented the ways in which children determined how any winnings were to be divided between capitalist and worker – apparently the larger share tended to go to the capitalist. Studies like this show that ways in which children can be engaging in mathematical thinking and learning in ways that may not be visible to teachers and parents.

A small number of studies have addressed the link between different forms of children's economic reasoning and behaviours and their mathematical thinking. For example, Taylor (2009) and Guberman (2004) focus on arithmetic operations involved in real-life monetary practices. Similarly, children have been shown to be capable of developing strategies to make effective economic decisions when saving (Otto et al., 2006) and parents actively teach their children to handle money autonomously (Furnham, 2001). It is important to note that children's economic activities are not restricted to those involving the handling of money, and non-monetary economic activities are also likely to involve mathematical thinking. For example, the exchanging of food in the playground (Nukaga, 2008), the negotiating of labour whilst playing (Webley, 1996) and the collecting of trading cards (Cook, 2001) all involve mathematical thinking.

In this project, we aimed to further explore children's out-of-school economic activity as a potential site for mathematical thinking and learning. We began by working with groups of children to document such out-of-school activity, and then followed this up by working with those same children to explore potential mathematical aspects to that activity. We did all of this with a view to supporting the building of connections for children between the mathematics that they were engaged with in an informal way outside of school and the mathematics that they experienced in the classroom.

Project Design

Compared with researching classroom activity, it is difficult to research children's out-of-school lives. Part of this difficulty is the fact that there can be a huge variety of activity happening in children's lives, even if we just focus on the activity that might involve mathematical thinking and learning (Hughes & Pollard, 2006). This in turn can mean that it is difficult to ensure that researchers and participants share definitions of terms and so effectively communicate the kinds of information that would be of most interest for the research. We have found that this is a particular problem when we use the term 'mathematics'. Children that we have worked with have very strong ideas about what counts as 'mathematics' and a very narrow conception of the kinds of out-of-school activity that might involve mathematical thinking. In informal conversations during the early stages of the project, we asked children, 'What mathematics do you do outside of school?' Every single time, the first answer that children gave involved counting money in a shop (aside from the answer 'maths homework', which a few children gave to begin with). Pupils either talked about making sure they had enough money to make a purchase or checking that they had been given the correct amount of change. After this, children generally struggled to come up with other ways in which they used maths outside the classroom. Those who could give another example usually talked about baking, and weighing flour in particular. What is interesting about these examples? What was interesting for us was the fact that these answers did not really seem to represent children's out-of-school lives. Rather, the descriptions of out-of-school maths resemble the kinds of representations of 'applied maths' that learners see in textbooks and worksheets. We thought that children probably had more interesting things going on in their lives than counting the amount of money in their pocket when in a shop, or weighing out flour, that involved mathematical thinking. After all, children are always being told how important maths is for both their future and for their day-to-day lives. But children were clearly struggling to think of ways in which activities they engaged in involved mathematical thinking, and ways in which mathematical thinking could help with the decision-making and problem-solving that these activities involve. So we decided to look at what children are doing outside the classroom that involves mathematical thinking, and to see what we could do to help children 'find the maths' in their day-to-day lives.

We therefore designed the project so that we could gradually build up our understanding of children's out-of-school activity, and the mathematical thinking and learning that might be involved, and then in turn better communicate to participants the kind of phenomena that we were interested in. The project proceeded in three phases; each informing the next.

Phase 1: Survey

A sample of 484 children was drawn from schools representing a range of demographic areas in Bristol. They were enroled in Year 5 ($n = 122$, Mean age = 10.06 years, 62 females), Year 7 ($n = 182$, Mean age = 12.43 years, 90 females) and Year 9 ($n = 180$, Mean age = 14.21 years, 96 females). The survey covered children's favourite possessions, pocket money practices, as well as monetary and non-monetary activity. One of the main purposes of the survey was to provide useful context for the rest of the project in terms of the kinds of activities we could expect children to report from their out-of-school lives and to begin to create a taxonomy of activities where we could expect to see evidence of informal mathematical thinking and learning.

Phase 2: Exploring Out-of-School Economic Activity

For us, this was the core of the project. We worked with primary and secondary schools in Bristol, supporting children to document their out-of-school economic activity and then bring these documents to small group interviews to explore the thinking and learning involved. In this part of the project we worked with children in Year 5 (9–10 years old) in two primary schools and Year 9 (13–14 years old) in one secondary school.

Phase 3: Bringing Home to School

The final phase of this project represented an opportunity to explore ways to make use of children's out-of-school activity and experience in the mathematics classroom. In this part of the project we focussed on children in the final year of primary school, who were 10–11 years old. Our aim here was to help children to 'find the maths' in their out-of-school lives.

Method and Main Findings

Phase 1: Survey

Children ranked technology (e.g. mp3 players), gaming items (e.g. consoles, games) and mobile phones amongst their most favourite possessions. Their access to money is rather limited. On average, children acquire £8.27 (SD = 9.08) per week, mostly in the form of pocket money from their parents. Children reported engaging with a diverse range of monetary activities, such as saving (70%), borrowing (60%), doing chores to earn money (65%), spending money (44%) and selling (33.9%). Non-monetary activities were also diverse. The most frequently reported included giving gifts (78.9%), borrowing things (51.4%), swapping (44.8%) and collecting (30.6%). Aggregated variables indexing children's spending money, monetary activity and non-monetary activity were calculated and processed with ANCOVAs including the factors Year and Gender, and a covariate that served as a proxy of socioeconomic level, namely the percentage of children enroled in the free school meal scheme of each school (FSM%). None of these factors or the covariate had an effect on the aggregates of spending money and monetary activity. The analysis of non-monetary activities revealed that girls reported more non-monetary activities than boys, and that Year 5 children reported more of these activities than those in Year 7 and Year 9. The results of the survey also showed that the participation of adults differentiated monetary activities and non-monetary activities. Although monetary activities such as spending, selling and saving could be carried out with autonomy, the money comes from parents (borrowed, or as earned or allowed pocket money), and is often transferred to other adults (e.g. in selling). In contrast, non-monetary activities were less related to adults and more related with peers. The results of the survey helped us to make decisions whilst designing the activities that were worth investigating. The survey suggested that a focus on children towards the younger end of the age range (10–11 years) would be valuable, as this seems to be an important time of transition where children are beginning to have autonomy in their economic decisions and are participating in a range of monetary and non-monetary activities.

Phase 2: Exploring Out-of-School Economic Activity

Following the survey carried out in phase 1, we were starting to become aware of the range of out-of-school activity that we could expect to see within our target participant group. However, we were also aware at this stage that further exploration of children's out-of-school activity further would be needed. While the survey had revealed the kinds of activities with which children engaged, it did not provide enough data to fully investigate the nature of children's thinking and learning during their engagement. In phase 2 of the project, then, we set out to collect a much richer set of data.

To find out more about children's economic activity, we worked with classes of children in three schools – two classes of Year 5 children and one class in Year 8 – over 3 weeks:

Week 1:   We gave children a structured diary to take home and complete over a period of 4 days, including a weekend. For each day, the diary contained a list of activities that we took from the survey findings. The first page listed activities involving money (e.g. spending money, putting money in a money box, working for money) and a second page listed activities that didn't involve money (e.g. adding to a collection, swapping something, borrowing something). There was space on each page for children to add activities that we hadn't listed. Children also took home a questionnaire for parents to complete.

Week 2:   Children returned their diaries, and talked in groups about similarities and differences they noticed in the set of activities they had recorded. We distributed 'documenting cards' to groups of children. These cards had an economic activity on one side: either an activity involving money – e.g. buying something, selling something, working for money, putting money in a money box or an activity not involving money – such as swapping something with a friend, adding to a collection, borrowing something, lending something. On the other side of the card there were some questions prompting children to think about the context in which the activity takes place. These questions were different for different activities, but often included questions about where the activity took place, who else was involved and what decisions needed to be made. Children talked together about the activities named on the cards and decided on two – one involving money and one not involving money – that they thought they were likely to engage in during the coming weekend. Each child took home the two cards that they had chosen, and a digital camera. They were asked to use the camera to take two or three photographs that they thought represented the activities that they had chosen to document.

Week 3:   Children brought the cameras and the completed documenting cards back to school. They then took part in small-group (3 or 4 children per group) discussions that focussed on the activities that they had documented. The first question we asked in these sessions was always, 'Can you tell us about one of the photographs you took?' Children could draw on the photographs and their completed cards during this activity. Both of these helped to break the barrier between school and home activity. Children told us about a huge range of activities – once they had described the activity they had documented, we were able to ask how that activity worked and also see if the experience of that activity was similar or different to that of other children in the group.

Phase 3: Bringing Home to School

Phase 2 of the project showed us that children's out-of-school economic activity represented a rich seam of resource for mathematical thinking and learning. While children were not initially aware of the mathematical content of tasks, discussions with groups about the nature of activities revealed some sophisticated planning, modelling and decision-making. One of the striking findings from this part of the project was the difficulty experienced by children in making connections between the mathematics in their everyday lives and the mathematics that they were familiar with from the classroom. The final phase of the project, then, set out to develop and test classroom activities to encourage children to make these connections. We worked with two Year 6 groups (10-to 11-year-old children) during this phase – both classes of 30 children, in two different primary schools.

Work with participants in this phase of the project began in the same way as it did in phase 2. In week 1, participants completed the same structured diaries as were used in phase 2. This encouraged them to develop an awareness of the range and frequency of economic activities in their out-of-school lives. In week 2, participants returned their completed diaries and took away digital cameras and documenting cards to document one or two examples of economic activity from their out-of-school lives. In week 3, we diverged from the previous plan. This time, rather than interview small groups of children ourselves, we asked children to work in pairs, and to interview one another about the activities that they had documented. We asked participants to think of themselves as journalists, and to find out as much as they could about their partner's activity. We provided some question prompts, such as asking about who else was involved, where the activity takes place and what kinds of decision-making was involved. Following this, participants were asked to complete a short workbook, entitled 'finding the maths', in which they were asked to record some of the mathematical thinking and learning involved in their activities.

Main Findings

There were three main areas of findings from phases 2 and 3 of the project. The first was a set of case studies of activities that we learnt about from our participants. The second was a comparison of the kinds of activities that children told us about across the three different schools. The third followed an analysis of children's responses to the classroom 'find the maths' activities that were introduced in phase 3. In the remainder of this chapter, we provide a summary of these findings and discuss the way in which they informed the next stage of our work.

To illustrate the kinds of activities that we were able to document within the project, we include an extract of data from one of the small-group discussion in phase 2. A group of four girls spoke to us about their experience of collecting trading cards associated with the *Doctor Who* television programme. The children talked about the ways that they built a collection – by spending money on packs of cards and by swapping cards within their friendship group. They told us about the ways in which the value of a particular card was determined, as a combination of the card's rarity and the popularity of the character pictured on the card. *K and C are two Year 6 girls, and R is a researcher.*

K: And then there's like commons, and then there'll be an ultra rare that's like really rare and you might trade that for another one

R: Can you tell me more about that?

C: There's common, rare, super rare and ultra rare

R: How do you know? Is that written on the cards?

K: Yeah, there's like a 'c' or 'r'. Also there's like in every series there's like... infinite card... which is

C: One in a thousand

K: Yeah one in a thousand packs

C: You can buy that on eBay for like twenty pounds, it's quite...

K: More than that. I checked on eBay it said seven, well with my dad, it said seventy pounds. I mean obviously no one would buy it for that but if someone was really desperate they probably would

R: So when you're collecting them, if you got a card you already had, would you swap that with somebody else?

C: Yeah, say if... we trade...

K: We mainly try and get rid of our doubles

C: We have to try and make it fair, so a common for a common or a rare for two commons or another rare. Or a super rare is for like four commons.

R: So how do you decide how many commons a rare is worth?

K: Well we... If we...

C: I don't know it's kind of revolved, I mean evolved

R: Evolved, right

K: Say if I had a common which is quite good like Amy Pond and then she's got um a rare that's rubbish then we might just swap them

C: It depends what the cards are

K: It depends how much someone wants it

C: We kind of do it like a super rare is worth three commons and a shiny, or two shinies

R: And the shinies...?

C: The shinies are rare

Within this segment we see explanations of relationships between rarity and value. There is an implicit recognition that while the rarity of a card is associated with its value, this relationship is not perfect and the value of a card is also determined by its desirability and the need for transactions to appear fair. There is some discussion of both trades within the game, involving swapping cards, and trades outside the game, where particularly rare or valuable cards are bought for money. Much of the conversation focussed on the social nature of the activity. The girls talked about the fact that they didn't think the cards were worth the amount that they spent on them. They had all started collecting the cards when the publishers released the first series of *Doctor Who* cards and were still collecting them now when they were on series three. They were well aware of the publisher's motives in releasing several series of the same kind of cards.

K: They keep changing to get more money out of you. There's like an old one – about five or ten years ago

C: Yeah about five or ten years ago there were these old cards that were quite good and there were loads of them. And then they changed to these new ones that we collect and then like after about six weeks they suddenly changed to another one. And we're like hang on we still haven't completed that one.

K: And then we start buying that one.

C: And there's special edition cards that you only get with a magazine

K: And us three we got these tins that you get and also you buy some magazines with them in and you get like these autographs

R: So can you still buy the old sets when the new ones come out?

C: No it's really annoying

Given this understanding, they had, as a group, tried to give up buying trading cards on more than one occasion. They had been able to stop buying cards for periods of time, but then when one girl in the group started collecting again, the others joined in.

C: But we don't collect them really any more. Because we've kind of realised because it's really expensive.

K: I've spent about more than fifty pounds. It's one pound fifty for like nine cards

C: At the end I said to myself I'm not going to collect any of these any more because they waste your money but we always start it again and we stopped this one and they said... And I just said oh this wastes my money but I bet we're going to come back into it

In this later part of the conversation we saw informal understanding of supply and demand, and of value for money. These ideas were all situated firmly in the context of collecting trading cards – which was described as a socially important activity.

Findings from Phase 3

This part of the project was instrumental in laying the foundations for the Everyday Maths project, as it demonstrated to us how difficult it is to support children in making connections between home and school through classroom work alone.

Phase 3 involved the research team designing classroom activity that required children to draw on their documentation of out-of-school activity to find and share examples of mathematical thinking and learning. Participating children completed the same documenting activities as in phase 2, but then their photographs were printed for them to use in a collaborative exercise with a partner. Children worked in pairs, interviewing one another to explore the mathematical thinking in the activities that they had documented. They were supported in this by a writing frame designed by the research team which prompted them with examples of questions and useful language. Data from the classroom work comprised completed writing frames plus audio recordings from discussions of a sample of pairs of children.

This phase of the project was an opportunity for us to test the likelihood of success of a classroom intervention to support children in making links between their out-of-school interests and activities and their experience of mathematics in the classroom. Children did not find this activity easy. All of the children enjoyed talking about the activities that they had documented, but many struggled to find ways in which these activities could be thought of in mathematical ways. We recorded a conversation between two children (F and G) that exemplifies the difficulties that many children faced:

F: What maths can you use when you're gift shopping?
G: You can use addition and calculation
F: So we could write, um, you could use multiplication and perimeter
G: Yes... perimeter? Why would you use perimeter?
F: How about weighing?
G: So you'd get one present because it was heavier than the other?
F: Maybe you'd need to use number bonds? So like four and six equals ten.
G: Ok so I've written we need addition, subtraction maybe if we go over. We need mental calculation
F: How about square numbers? [long pause]

In this example, the children attempted to build explanations around particular words that they thought were 'mathematical' (in the data above, these were words like addition, calculation, perimeter, number bonds, square numbers). This, however, created a problem when the words chosen did not lend themselves to the task. This can be compared with the examples in the previous study, where the focus of conversations was on the activity rather than the mathematics, and these kinds of 'mathematical words' were never used. Children clearly found it difficult to negotiate between the language of the mathematics classroom and the language of their out-of-school lives.

We did see positive responses to the task. Some children expressed surprise about their ability to see some of their activities in mathematical ways and wrote positively about the ways in which they thought that maths could help them with their out-of-school activities. One boy wrote about the mathematics involved in understanding football players' performance statistics as part of a football manager computer game, and in understanding football league tables and the permutations of possible outcomes during end-of-season playoffs, for example.

Chapter Summary

This chapter has described an exploratory study of children's out-of-school mathematical thinking and learning. While not aiming to generate a comprehensive account of all mathematical thinking and learning that children engage with outside of school, the series of studies carried out within the project did demonstrate a variety and depth of mathematical activity. The focus on the mathematical thinking in economic activity (broadly defined) revealed a wide range of activities and provided opportunities for the research team to discuss activities in some depth with children.

In phase 2 of the project, we saw that while children are clearly using informal mathematical thinking in a great deal of their out-of-school activity, such informal mathematics is thought of as very different to the formal mathematics that they know from the classroom. Even where the research team could see very clear analogies between reported out-of-school activities and the KS2 mathematics curriculum[1], children spoke about their out-of-school activities using notably different language compared to when they spoke about classroom mathematics. While discussion regarding out-of-school activity were focussed on practical decision-making and problem-solving grounded in the experience of that activity, discussions about classroom maths focussed on lists of terms (e.g. fractions, decimals, percentages) and definitions. Our interpretation of our findings was that there is work to be done in helping children identify ways in which the mathematics they learn in the classroom can be useful in the wider context of life and work, as their conception of mathematics in this study was that it was very much restricted to use within a mathematics lesson in school.

In phase 3 of the project we attempted to broaden children conceptions of mathematics by supporting them in bringing their own documents (as in phase 2) representing out-of-school activity and then working together to 'find the maths' in such activity. This met with mixed levels of success – while some children took to this activity well and made some useful connections, the majority found it extremely difficult to talk about any links between classroom mathematics and their out-of-school activity. We concluded that children are likely to need close adult facilitation and support to make such connections between the mathematics they encounter in their everyday lives and the mathematics of the classroom effectively. We also acknowledged (in line with Hughes & Pollard, 2006) that it would be difficult for a teacher to fulfil this role effectively with a class of 30 children all with a unique set of out-of-school interests.

Taken as a whole, the project told us that children's out-of-school activities represent a rich resource for mathematical learning, but that this resource is generally underused. While it would be rather challenging for a teacher to manage support for children to make connections between the classroom and all of the variety of activity in which they engage outside of school, we concluded that there was an opportunity for others to work with children in this way. The natural group to move to next, for us, was parents. Parents are generally not experts in mathematics education, but do tend to be experts in their children's lives (for our target children of up to around 10 years of age, at least) and do have a strong interest in supporting their children's learning. This brings us to our next chapter.

Chapter 4

The Everyday Maths Project

Introduction

The Everyday Maths project (2013–2015) focussed on the kinds of mathematics that families do in their everyday lives. The project aimed to develop our understanding of home–school partnerships and of how parents support their children's maths learning at home. Through the project, we wanted to develop ways to empower parents in supporting their children's maths learning. By empower, we mean that we wanted to help parents become confident to recognise that they had expertise that could support their children's learning and could make their own choices about how to do so. We recognised that parents, for a variety of reasons outlined in Chapter 2, struggle to support their children's school maths learning, so we wanted to help families to become more confident in their relationships with mathematics. Building on the Economic Activity project, the Everyday Maths project worked on the principles that: parents want to support their children's learning; there is potential to draw on family activity to help do this and parents are positioned better than teachers to use family activity as a starting point, as they know about their children's home lives (at least when their children are in primary school). We believed that improving parents' confidence would enable them to have more supportive interactions with their children around the mathematics that occurred in everyday family activity. While we ultimately hoped that the project would have an impact on pupil attainment, this was not the main focus of our work: we were concerned about parental confidence and the nature of parental relationships with mathematics.

As a research team, our own backgrounds, interests and mathematical confidence were important to how the project developed: we discuss this below and in other chapters. The research team was made up of Tim, Jo and Ben. Tim is a psychologist and ex-maths teacher with a research interest in maths learning and considerable expertise in maths. He is a father of one child. Jo is a social psychologist with research interests in collaborative partnerships and inclusive education. Although Jo did not study maths beyond first-year undergraduate level, she is confident in her mathematical ability and enjoys tangling with mathematical concepts. She is not a parent. Ben is an educational researcher with research interests around children with special educational needs and their families. At the

Parental Engagement and Out-of-School Mathematics Learning, 31–48
Copyright © 2023 Tim Jay and Jo Rose
Published under exclusive licence by Emerald Publishing Limited
doi:10.1108/978-1-78769-705-820231004

start of the project, Ben had little confidence in his own mathematical ability. He is the father of two children.

We used González et al.'s (2005) concept of funds of knowledge as a starting point, recognising that families already hold considerable expertise (in our case, mathematical expertise) that is used in everyday activity. This expertise, however, is not necessarily structured in the same way as formal school curriculum knowledge and may not be recognised as belonging to that curriculum subject. The types of spontaneous mathematical activity that children engage in during their everyday lives were demonstrated in the Economic Activity project, as discussed in Chapter 3. In the Everyday Maths project, we built on this to focus on the range of activities that parents and children discussed or engaged in together.

The Everyday Maths project was initially conceptualised as a relatively straightforward programme of research, working with around 20 primary schools across Bristol. We intended to conduct a survey followed by focus groups in every school, to explore parents' perspectives on their children's maths learning and their role in supporting that learning. This would then inform a series of six workshops with parents, in four of the primary schools. We hoped that the workshops would help parents explore ways in which they could support their children's maths learning by drawing on their funds of knowledge from home or work. The final aspect of the research was to conduct an ongoing evaluation of these workshops to understand their impact (particularly on parental confidence) and how they could be transferred to other settings. We hoped that the workshops would be useful for parents, teachers and children, that schools would want to continue with the workshops beyond our intervention and that other schools would be interested in running the workshops themselves. Ultimately we hoped that through such activities, children's motivation, interest and achievement in mathematics would be raised – although this was not the focus of our research.

In the Everyday Maths project, we initially aimed to work with parents of children in Years 3 and 4 (ages 7/8 and 8/9 years old). At this point, school mathematics as structured by the National Curriculum (Department for Education, 2013) has moved beyond basic arithmetic and involves developing fluency in arithmetic calculations, using mathematical vocabulary, and developing mathematical reasoning. This could then be the point at which some parents would begin to feel more anxious about supporting their children. Many parents – even those with low confidence and basic levels of mathematical ability – are likely to feel that they understand Key Stage 1 mathematics (when children are 5/6 and 6/7 years old). As the curriculum progresses, however, parental anxiety may develop. We were particularly interested in working with parents who did not feel confident with school mathematics as it progressed beyond basic arithmetic.

This chapter will discuss our experiences and challenges in the implementation of the Everyday Maths project and outline our core findings. Further chapters will explore in more depth the themes arising from the Everyday Maths project, also drawing on the Economic Activity project.

The Bristol Context

Bristol is the largest city in the South West of England, with around 450,000 people. There is a diverse population with different areas of the city having distinctive characteristics. The 2011 Census (as summarised by Mills, 2012) showed 78% of Bristol's population as being of White British ethnicity, with 16% from Black and minority ethnic groups, and 6% from other White ethnicities. The proportion of Black and minority ethnic groups in the population in the 2011 Census had almost doubled since the 2001 Census. Around 85% of the population were born in the United Kingdom, with the remaining 15% being born in another country – the proportion of immigrants in the 2011 Census had also nearly doubled since 2001. Around 33% of the population in 2011 were educated to degree level or above, and 20% had no qualifications. Figures from 2015 show that around 17% of the population were living in income deprivation (Mills, 2015), although this varies widely with around 49% of people in the most deprived wards living in income deprivation, to less than 1% in the least deprived wards. Bristol, then, has different areas with distinct characteristics in terms of population – with wide variation between areas in terms of income and employment, educational levels, ethnicity and so on. This provides an interesting context to work with schools and parents. Our understanding of the demographics of different areas, and of schools within those areas, informed our recruitment for the project. At each stage, we aimed to recruit schools which served a range of different areas, with different levels of attainment and with different proportions of ethnic minority and English as an Additional Language (EAL) children in the schools.

Designing and Conducting the Survey

The first element of the project was the survey. We intended to design the surveys to understand parents' attitudes towards their children's mathematics learning and what they believed their role in this to be. We had expected that this would help us understand how confident parents were in supporting their children's maths learning. Specifically, we aimed to measure the extent to which parents engaged in their children's maths learning, levels of motivation that parents had to help their child's mathematics learning and parents' perceptions of how well equipped they were to support this. As discussed in Chapter 2, core factors that can hinder parental engagement with their children's maths learning include: parental ability (or at the very least, perceived parental ability or confidence) in mathematics; parents' familiarity with the specific methods that their children are learning at school (often parents feel that mathematics is taught differently to how they were taught at school) and parents' confidence in helping their child learn (how to 'act as a teacher'). The extent to which parents believe it is their role or the school's role to educate their child is a likely predictor of parental involvement (Hoover-Dempsey et al., 2005). Further, the ability or achievement level of the child may also impact on how a parent feels about supporting their child and the way in which they approach this – so we felt that it was important to understand this as part of the context.

These constructs presented us with several problems to untangle. We wanted surveys to be anonymous, and non-threatening, to encourage parents to respond. In an ideal world, part of understanding how well-equipped parents felt in supporting their children would entail asking questions about parental achievement in mathematics. A parent with a degree in mathematics or which involved a substantial mathematical component, for example, might feel better equipped to support their children's maths learning than a parent who had failed their GCSE in mathematics. We were aware, though, that this would be potentially threatening for parents – especially those may have not done well in mathematics at school themselves. The less confident parents were those we were most interested in working with going forward, so we did not want to risk putting them off further participation through misjudged survey questions.

Our response to this was to ask parents about their confidence, engagement and enjoyment in mathematics (Question 11), along with their level of general education (Question 13). While this did not give us an exact measure of parental attainment in mathematics, it gave us a range of measures which we could use to assess parents' relationships with mathematics.

Moving to children's attainment, it is possible that not all parents would know (or want to share) their child's attainment in mathematics, and if they did share this then it would likely not be in a standardised format. We wanted surveys to be anonymous, so matching surveys to school attainment data was not an option, even if we had obtained the necessary permissions and if data were in the same format across all schools. Understanding the level at which children were working in mathematics, then, proved to be problematic. Our decision here was to ask parents about their child's preference for maths and their child's performance in maths compared to other children in their class. This proved problematic for one school, however, as they had a policy to actively dissuade parents from comparing their children to others in the school and thinking about their children's relative positions in the class. As a result we were not able to collect the data at that school.

We were also concerned about making a distinction between engagement/ attainment in mathematics and engagement/attainment in other school subjects – it may be, for example, that children are engaged in maths learning, but not dramatically more so than in other subjects. For example, two children could spend similar amounts of time on mathematics outside of school, but for one child this is the only type of school work they do outside of school, and for the second child they spend as much time (or more) on other subjects. This might indicate that the first child had more of a preference for mathematics over other subjects than the second child. As a result, when we asked about children's interactions with mathematics, we asked similar questions about other subjects and about learning in general (Questions 1–8).

We ended up with a survey that would provide us with relevant information, but our constructs and measures were not as clearly defined as we would like. The survey was brief and anonymous as we were trying to maximise response rates, and we asked participating schools to distribute it for us along with a cover letter explaining the project. Following low response rates, we also attended schools ourselves at home time, to distribute the survey to parents. Ultimately, our response rate was too low ($n = 243$, across 18 schools) to conduct any meaningful statistical analysis of the data. Descriptive summaries of the data, however, demonstrated that the majority of parents felt that they had a responsibility to help their children with their schoolwork. Across measures of parent confidence, around 1/3 of parents were not confident about their ability to help their child in learning maths. It was clear, then, that a substantial minority of parents had low levels of confidence in supporting their children's out-of-school maths learning and may therefore have been interested in our workshops. Importantly, the survey also gave us entrance into schools – this was the first step in a multistage research project and it allowed us to start to develop relationships with parents.

Focus Groups With Parents

Following on from the surveys, we ran several focus groups with parents to add to our understanding of parental attitudes and confidence (see Jay et al., 2018). These were more helpful than the surveys in many ways: the content of the data was more revealing; the recruitment process helped us understand more about how our participant schools worked; and we were able to further develop our research relationships with parents and with the school administration.

Following our limited success with the survey response rate, in the run-up to the focus groups we spent more time in school playgrounds at drop-off and pick-up times, introducing ourselves to parents and chatting with them about the project. We explained that we were interested in understanding how they talked with their children about mathematics learning, as this would help us understand how parents can be supported to develop more confidence in this. Attendance at focus groups varied widely between schools – from two to 15 parents, although usually around five or six parents turned up. In one school (in which we subsequently ran workshops), only one parent turned up, so instead we took a more informal approach of short conversations with parents in the playground at pick-up time, broadly discussing the focus group topics. We were interested that some schools believed that parents of their pupils would not get involved, and positioned parents as very difficult to engage. This signalled that school/parent relationships were not necessarily extensive or in-depth, and aligned with parental anxieties about school-centred involvement that will be discussed below.

The broad topics covered in the focus groups included: the ways in which parents interacted with their children about mathematics; parents' experiences of school mathematics and how that differs from their children's experiences; interaction with school about mathematics; parents' confidence and feelings about mathematics and about helping their children with mathematics; and ways in which parents use mathematics in their everyday lives.

We discuss in Chapter 2 the distinction between school-centred parental involvement in children's learning (involvement which is in service of the school's agenda and focuses on relationships between schools and parents) and home-centred parental involvement (spontaneous or planned activities that focus on learning and that do not stem from school suggestions), similar to the distinction between parental involvement and parental engagement that was highlighted by Goodall and Montgomery (2014). Parents in our focus groups discussed anxieties around their own confidence in mathematics, in their familiarity with the mathematics used in their children's school and around acting as a teacher of their child, for example (*R is the researcher, P is a parent*).:

R: Do you think you've got the skills to write out these sums and mark these sums?

P1: Simple ones, I do. I'm not as good as his dad, so as I said, his dad isn't connecting how they work it out with the way I work it out, so [my son] says 'You're confusing me Mum!' And I'm like alright I'll step back. But I mean, I can give him basic sums, but I'm used to school in Jamaica because I remember more of school in Jamaica than I do here. Also some things he works out, and I think 'You worked that out quicker than I would!' I don't understand how he got here. He's like 'Minus that and that', and I'm like you know what? I don't know. I would like to learn a lot more ways.

None of this was a surprise given that this is well established in the literature (Peters et al., 2008). The focus groups highlighted the ways in which parents experienced school-centred involvement: parents felt uncomfortable with differences between their expertise and what was expected from their children, and felt that they did not have enough guidance from schools on how best to support their children's homework:

P2: Yeah, so that they could understand because obviously it wasn't going to be helpful for me to explain how I worked it out because that's not the way they were learning it. So it would have been more confusing to say, 'This the way I've done it', and they'd be like, 'What are you doing?' So it was more just, obviously you can't turn off the switch and you don't want to turn off the switch of the way that you do it because you know how to do it, but it's just trying to show them the process. In fact, I had to show, I had to work out the process for myself first and I think, 'That's a crap way of doing it', but that's only because that your brain has been trained in a certain way to do it, it's not really, is it?

and

P3: I think the way I was taught at school, from going to that workshop I think they will be taught but I think we just missed out a lot of stages in between. So now my daughter will come, did come home a while ago saying, 'We're doing partitioning', she wanted to practise at home and I didn't know what she meant. And in the end she managed to explain it to me.

This appeared to present barriers to their involvement, and may explain why attempts to raise children's attainment through schools working to increase parental involvement generally show few positive outcomes. Discussions around more parent-centred involvement, however, were more positive. Parents spoke about wanting to ensure that their children developed positive attitudes towards mathematics, and about the ways different members of the family (older siblings, for example, as well as parents) could learn alongside children as they supported them in their school work.

> P4: Yes, my daughter teaches me. Teaches me to teach him, sometimes she teaches him there because (inaudible 00:20:55) for more, she's in year 10 this year. So she's lots of homework ...
> P5: And she likes mathematics as well?
> P4: Yes, she is really good at maths, yes.

When asked, parents also offered examples of mathematical thinking they used with their children outside of school work – this included counting and categorising, using money, talking about time, and food and cooking (measuring and mixing ingredients, timings, working out portion sizes and so on):

> P6: Well, he'll sort of say to me, you know how long is dinner and I might say it is at 6 o'clock and he says well how long is that and I say to him you need to have a look and try to work it out, things like that or he might say to me, this morning for instance, he said to me you owe me £1.20. Then he says I need £2 so I can buy Pokemon cards and I say how much more do you need then and how many weeks of pocket money until you get it. We'll have those sorts of conversations.

and

> P7: Thinking right, we've got to sit here for half an hour and he'll be getting itchy and so I remember like one day just taking my purse out and I'd got all my money or whatever and I was saying, 'Ooh, can you make £1.53?' or 'Can you make whatever', and so he just sat there doing different amounts and pretending and adding it up and so it's more that type, it's not like a, 'Here, go and do your maths thing', it's more just, 'Oh yeah we have, we are actually doing maths but we're not', it's only to keep him happy to be honest.

Although this kind of activity did not appear to have such negative emotions attached to it, the conversations about this type of activity were more hesitant and stilted than those about homework – which suggests that parents are not always aware of the ways they use mathematics in everyday life and struggle to describe it. Many of the examples used were framed as if in mathematics text books (cooking, money and time, to illustrate standard arithmetic functions). As with children in the Economic Activity project, it appears that parents found it difficult to step outside of thinking about mathematics as a curriculum subject taught in school.

The focus groups, then, fulfilled a number of functions. Firstly, we started to engage with parents in schools at a more personal level and develop research relationships with them beyond them just completing a questionnaire. The time spent hanging around in playgrounds, as well as actually conducting the focus groups, was invaluable for 'getting our faces known', so parents felt comfortable around us. The process of setting up and running the focus groups, and the content of parents' discussions, helped us recognise that formal workshops to develop parents' capacities to support their children's learning would not be a good idea. For parents to feel comfortable and open up to us, we needed a more informal atmosphere. Parents struggled to discuss mathematics in ways that were not closely related to standard curriculum mathematics, so workshops that were reminiscent of a school classroom with researchers in the teacher role would risk closing down parents' participation. When considering the workshops' focus, we acknowledged that parents struggled with communication from schools about their children's maths learning. If the workshops focussed on helping parents to interpret school mathematics, however, this would not lead to lasting change: we would only be able to address specific curriculum-related questions as they arose and parents would be entirely dependent on us to help them. Their children's curriculum would constantly evolve as they progressed through school, and we wouldn't always be there to try to help parents interpret and engage with it. Instead, we needed to develop parents' confidence that they already had expertise to support their children's learning in different ways – and running formal classes on school mathematics, with us in the role of teachers, would not be a good way to approach this. We needed an informal, conversational style of workshop which could give parents the opportunity to recognise their expertise and lead the conversations.

Planning the Workshops

The workshops were originally planned as a series of six workshops over the course of the school year, to help parents develop confidence in their ability to support their children's maths learning. Following our experiences in the Economic Activity project, and the content of the focus groups, we understood that the focus should not be on school or curriculum mathematics – but also that it might be difficult to move parents' expectations away from this. Further, following our experiences of (1) persuading parents to attend focus groups and (2) parents' reluctance to engage with anything too formal, we felt that we had to be flexible and responsive to parents' needs if the workshops were to be successful. We could not say for sure there would be six workshops, and we could not be too rigid about the purpose of the workshops.

We ran the workshops in four schools, all of whom had participated in the focus groups. These schools were selected partly because of interest from parents and the school and partly because they had very different demographics. Between them, they had a range of percentages of children eligible for free school meals (a common indicator of deprivation), percentages of children with EAL and average attainment at Key Stage Two (national tests of English and Maths when pupils are aged 10/11 years old). At one of the schools, only one parent turned up to the focus group and we ended up speaking with parents in the playground instead of running formal focus groups. We were keen to work with this school, as well as some where parents demonstrated more confidence and enthusiasm in engaging with research. It was important for us to reflect on how we could position the workshops to be attractive to a wide range of parents, beyond those who were already active participants in school-based events.

The characteristics of the four schools are presented in Table 1. Pseudonyms are used for the schools, and exact figures are not used to preserve schools' anonymity.

As a project team, we had several conversations to refine the purpose of the workshops, considering how to make them useful for parents and also helpful for our own research agenda. We also needed to reflect on the process of the workshops, and plan how to run them. We each brought our own experiences, values and ideas to these conversations. Tim's interest in mathematics learning, Jo's interest in how parents work together and Ben's interest in family relationships all contributed to the shape of the workshop plans. These interests all combined to

Table 1. School Characteristics for Those Participating in the Everyday Maths Workshops.

School	Level of Pupils on Free School Meals	Level of Pupils With English as an Additional Language	Attainment at Key Stage 2 (% Pupils Achieving at Least Level 4 in All of Maths, Reading and Writing)
Crossways	Low: Around half the national average	Low: Around half the national average	Higher than the national average
Riverside	Extremely high: Around five times the national average	Extremely high: Around five times the national average	Lower than the national average
Wood Close	High: Around twice the national average	Very high: around three times the national average	Similar to the national average
Queens Street	Very high: around three times the national average	High: around twice the national average	Lower than the national average

inform what became our main agenda: understanding parental relationships with mathematics.

Prior to the workshops we developed outline plans, although these were responsive to parents' reactions within the workshop sessions and the workshops played out very differently in different schools. During and in between the different workshop sessions, we had to think on our feet and develop ideas as we went along. We spent a lot of time in between workshops discussing our experiences and the next steps within the workshops. As the workshops progressed and our relationships with parents developed, it became clear that six sessions would be too many. Our plan centred around an introductory session followed by four workshops. The project, then, took the shape it did because of who we were as individuals and our relationships as a team, and because of the characteristics of the parents participating in the workshops. With a different project team and/or with different parents participating, it is very likely that the workshops would have taken a very different shape. Describing the workshops does not communicate the messiness and ad hoc nature of the process, but in order to present them clearly, we need to simplify what happened to some extent. What follows is a tidied-up approximation of the actual events!

Running the Workshops

The overall agenda of the workshops was as follows:

(1) Introductory session.
(2) Workshop 1: Thinking about everyday family activity
(3) Workshop 2: Finding the maths
(4) Workshop 3: Thinking about conversations with children
(5) Workshop 4: Reflecting on the workshop process (evaluation)

Following discussions with parents, we ran the workshop sessions at 9 a.m. in the morning, after drop-off time. This did not suit all parents, but parents felt that after school would be problematic due to child care. Starting at 9 a.m. meant that those who could make it did not have to make a special trip in and could just stay on at school after dropping their child off. Workshops were run with around four weeks in between each one (although of the introductory session was only one or two weeks before the first workshop). In hindsight this was too far apart: the workshops would probably work best in quicker succession, with one or two weeks in between each one to keep up momentum and enable easier follow-on from one conversation to the next.

Introductory Session

In all schools we held a pre-workshop session where we described to parents the principles of what we were doing, answered questions and tried to work out what time of day would suit most people. In the introductory session, some parents came to us asking for help with their child's mathematics homework. This demonstrated parents' focus on mathematics as a curriculum subject (rather than everyday activity), although perhaps this should not be surprising given that we were based in the school. At the introductory session, and in workshop 1, we emphasised that we were aiming to step away from school mathematics and wanted to support parents to recognise that they did mathematics in their everyday lives. We explained that parents did not need to be experts in the school curriculum to be able to support their children's mathematics learning.

Workshop 1: Thinking About Everyday Family Activity

We wanted parents to feel comfortable taking the lead in workshops, with us taking the role as facilitators, not teachers. To do so, we wanted the first workshop to be about things that parents would find it easy to talk about and that we (as facilitators) didn't know about so could not take the lead on. Drawing on our experiences in the Economic Activity project, we started with everyday family activity. For some parents, asking what they did at the weekend with their children was challenging – it can be hard to articulate everyday things like having breakfast, doing the washing, watching television and so on, and not many families do 'special activities' at the weekend that might seem noteworthy. Others found it hard to step outside pre-existing ideas of what 'Everyday Maths' looked like and shared the kinds of activity that might be used in mathematics text books, such as shopping (including working out how much money and how much change was needed) or baking (weighing ingredients). This is not surprising given that we introduced the workshops as the 'Everyday Maths' project. Other parents, however, were more comfortable with chatting about what they had done with their children and gave a range of examples such as cleaning teeth, doing the washing up, sorting washing, gardening, playing games, going to the zoo, going swimming, going to the park and so on. We asked parents to come back to the second workshop ready to share further activities they had done as a family. To help them have prompts for discussion, we gave them digital cameras to record activity, notebooks and pens – stressing that they did not have to use them, but if they wanted to use them to record activity they could. In hindsight, this was not a good idea: some parents did not return to the second workshop, and their friends told us that they felt embarrassed because they had not done the 'homework'. We had tried to emphasise that they did not have to use notebooks, but this was a useful lesson to us in that we had to be careful in order make sure the workshops were not 'like school' – asking them to complete 'between-workshop tasks' was clearly problematic.

Workshop 2: Finding the Maths

In this workshop we aimed to use the examples of activity that parents had brought in, and discuss the potential for mathematical thinking in that activity. Some parents came in with photos and drawings or notes of activities they had done with their children. Others did not bring prompts or records but arrived with examples of activity they were happy to talk about. Parents discussed activities including straightforward arithmetic examples (similar to those raised in Workshop 1) and everyday activities such as making meals, sorting washing, cleaning teeth and so on, playing games such as snakes and ladders and Jenga, going out in the rain, going swimming, a walk in the park and so on. It was at this point that anxieties about the need to remain similar to school maths came to the fore:

> P8: And I guess you could, if you wanted to, do some arithmetic to actually work out the gradient. You could actually sit down and say 'Well, actually let's lay this out as a triangle; let's take a bit of the hill and see what the slope is now'. The problem is what could you use that for? I was going to say it would be nice if you could sort of help find a way of estimating the height of the hill or something like that that would be interesting, but you haven't got either number have you so...

Parents seemed to feel that it was important to structure their talk with children around what they defined as maths: the name 'Everyday Maths' apparently set boundaries around what parents felt they should focus on. They seemed uncomfortable crossing boundaries between maths and, for example, science, history, geography or art as defined by school curricula.

> P8: And then trying to explain what the gap is, yeah. I did also try the whole... 'If you stand up the top of the slope and you lift your feet why is it that it goes?' So I tried the idea that the rope is pulling you that way and your weight is pulling you that way, so the vector stuff basically. Yeah ... you're converting potential energy, aren't you and (inaudible 0:03:36) physics so are we allowed to do that, because that's not maths anymore is it?

This of course led to discussions with parents around the relationships between different areas of the curriculum and the extent to which it mattered that they were clearly delineated. Parents' thoughts about what does and does not count as maths, and how it is defined by them, will be explored further in later chapters.

Workshop 3: Thinking About Conversations With Children

In Workshop 3, we moved on to discussing the kinds of conversations parents had with their children about maths. In this workshop, parents were still anxious about differentiating topics according to the curriculum, and additionally raised their concerns around having natural conversations that included mathematical thinking.

> R: Whether or not you need school terms in order to grasp and understand the maths and talk about maths. So we talked about

velocity then was quite an interesting thing or addition and subtraction and estimating probability, whether or not these were kind of needed as part of the conversation; and I really don't know. Do you think it's possible to talk to your daughter without...?

P9: I think I should do with her because I think with [my son] he's not been too bad and I've not really had to think about it but with her that doesn't like maths, because she struggles with it I think that might be... I'm going to have to think more about, as you say, bringing it in so it's not maths or she doesn't think she's doing it.

Some parents struggled with conversations seeming too deliberate: they felt as if they forced maths into the conversation and their children recognised this, and either became irritated or switched off.

P10: Yeah. And what words can we use to sort of –

P11: When do we jump in and... yeah.

P10: Yeah so that we're sort of using the right maths-related language –

P11: Without making them feel like it is maths.

P10: Yeah. And questioning, that's it, so that it's just like planting seed: 'Yeah, where is the pattern in that?' And even if they can sit with that and not really – they can mull it over even if they don't answer you at first because they're involved in their thing.

P11: Yeah, because sometimes they're so involved in it they don't want to see.

P10: Yeah, but you're sort of feeding in the right language or the right ideas for them ... But then it's like at what point do you say 'Maths', do you identify it as maths?

P11: Because they sit there for a long time, how long do you let it go on for and then you say 'Yeah...' What should you say at the end?

This was where parents were really able to support each other: they are experts on their children and shared ideas to share around how they managed the parent/child dynamic.

P12: I've just thought of another one because I didn't get to speak before but to do with day and night: my children were asking me this morning how many hours there were in a day, and I said '24 hours' and then they said 'But how many hours are there in a night?' And then I was explaining to them when the day was and when the night was and how many hours that worked... and then it was different at different times – they really tripped me up. So we had to pick that apart on the way to school. I don't think we finished that conversation actually.

Some discussed how they took an approach of being interested in and excited by the world, and noticing interesting things. These conversations led parents to discuss particular issues: whether it was important to explicitly label ideas as maths – again picking up on anxieties around school-defined curricula:

> P13: I feel sometimes I want to have a definition of what maths is to be able to define and describe what it is, and I don't feel that I can.
>
> P14: Yeah. I suppose I haven't really been sort of consciously doing it as much as I would've liked. I think I'm often aware of how much of the strange... the sort of difference between maths and English; they have the same sort of status in school but they're so different the way that they are in our lives and... with stories and everything we spend a lot of time kind of around the language side of things without thinking too much about it but it's not the same for maths. So yeah I mean that's why we're here isn't it? It's more of a challenge to bring it into that sort of normal every day.

This led to discussions around whether it was important to have a specific agenda about what could come out of the conversation; whether it was important to produce 'answers' (or more specifically, 'right answers')

> P14: You wish the children did the maths that was relevant to the world rather than trying to make the world relevant to the maths they're doing.

or whether just noticing, wondering and exploring ideas and phenomena was enough:

> P13: I kind of like that time of spending time with your kids and – I mean whittling wood is far too creative for me, I'm still very ones and zeros and black and white, but I do really enjoy that thing of being with a child and like 'Wow, this is an amazing experience isn't it? How are we going to make – oh look, feel this. Actually I have got a bunch of concepts that I've kind of learnt from school that you haven't come across yet but let's stick with how you're experiencing this' and then maybe slowly I can say 'Well, look have you noticed there's a kind of shape to this. We call this a square'.

The conversations between parents, then, were important in highlighting specific preconceptions and uneasiness about discussing maths with their children – but also in helping parents to come to terms with uncertainty and allow themselves to have learning conversations with their children that were not directly focussed on the school curriculum.

> P12: Yeah sometimes just by adding a little more things we can make our child learn, just adding a few things to whatever we are discussing. That is a normal discussion but just asking a few more questions.

This highlighted that starting with activity (rather than with the maths) was important. It also highlighted that if parents could give themselves permission to not have to find a 'correct answer', but instead to just explore ideas and questions, they could move away from the anxiety of needing to be a maths expert and take ownership of supporting their children's learning.

R: That's why I got really excited when you were saying what you were saying about experiencing the world. To me that's the key of it and I've never thought about it like that before.

P13: And if we, as parents, can sort of get our heads around that and how maths and all of this is about helping them to refine their senses, the direct experience of the world.

R: It's kind of helping them experience the world, isn't it and reflect on that experience of the world, which is a kind of formalised way of what you were saying earlier about the (inaudible 0:50:08) in the wall and the signs; it's helping them to reflect on what they're seeing.

P13: Yeah, just seeing how they're thinking as well because you're sometimes thinking something else and they can see something that you haven't seen before, or the other way around. So you're trying to make them see something else but they've seen something else, and you think 'Wow, I didn't realise that was there' and that's maths too. But you don't want to say it's maths because some of them are scared of maths.

Workshop 4: Review, Reflect and Future Plans

We used the fourth session to reflect with parents on the process of the workshop: what was useful, what parents could take away and whether the workshops were transferable to other contexts with other facilitators. These sessions appeared to be useful for the parents, in terms of consolidating and naming the way their thinking had changed. The sessions were useful for us too, as researchers, in terms of helping us recognise and articulate the development that had taken place through the workshops, and also in helping us reflect on our role as facilitators.

During the workshops we had several voice recorders which we asked parents to switch on in groups if they were comfortable to do so, and these were later transcribed (not all groups recorded their conversations – some said that they felt uncomfortable and some said that they forgot). We also had our own field notes that we made during and after the workshop, and from some workshops, we had mind maps that parents drew on flip charts (paper, pens, Post-its were available at every workshop for use, if parents found them helpful). A fuller account of the workshops and key themes that arose can be found in Jay et al.'s (2017) work.

The Way the Workshops Played out in Different Schools

While the overview of the workshops presented above seems relatively straightforward, the boundaries between the different workshops were blurred, and they played out in different ways in different schools. In Crossways Primary School, which had low levels of free school meals and EAL, and high average levels of attainment, parents were confident and needed little scaffolding or support. Most of these parents were highly educated and came to the workshop with high levels of confidence in supporting their children's learning. They were willing to discuss their approaches and keen to add to their repertoire. By the second workshop parents had grasped the concept of discussing mathematical ideas that arose in activity and were happy trying this out with their children: these parents needed only minor prompts and were then happy to take ideas and run with them.

In Riverside Primary School, there was a contrasting demographic, with very high levels of free school meals and EAL, and low average levels of attainment. The majority of parents attending the workshop were relatively recent immigrants from one particular country. They were very motivated to support their children to do well at school, to the extent that they were buying in maths tutors for themselves so they could help their children with school maths, despite having low levels of income. This enthusiasm for supporting their children meant that they engaged with ideas discussed in workshops and were keen to pick up ideas from other parents. Their background in a dramatically different culture and education system, however, meant that many ideas were new to them: some parents explained, for example, how they had not considered ideas such as counting steps with their children. The workshops, then, played out in a different way to those in Crossways Primary School: the emphasis was more on number and basic arithmetic, such as that covered in the early years of primary school. While such interaction with their children may seem obvious to parents who had been through the English education system (and done well in that system themselves), the parents we met at Riverside Primary School had not come across these ideas before. This highlights the advantages that parents from particular backgrounds (particularly those with experience of the education system and those who have done well in that education system) have when it comes to supporting their children.

In Wood Close Primary School there was a mixed demographic in terms of parents' level of education and confidence in engaging with maths. Despite the school having very high levels of EAL children, the majority of parents we worked with were native English speakers from a range of backgrounds. In this school, only one parent turned up to the focus group, but we had good levels of engagement through the workshops. The specific sub-group we worked with in the workshops (i.e. native English speakers) indicates potential differences in the ways parents from different backgrounds may feel comfortable or able to be involved. Parents seemed to enjoy the gradual process of coming to think differently about maths and about the school curriculum, and demonstrated a shift in their thinking over the duration of the four workshops. This shift seemed to result from the conversations that took place over time and probably would not have been achieved with fewer sessions.

In Queen Street Primary School we worked with parents from a wide range of countries, none of whom had English as a first language. These parents were curious and motivated to help their children, but seemed to be very anxious around school activity. The relationships and dynamics of the group seemed particularly important in this school: the way in which the conversations progressed and individual parents' confidence seemed to vary according to the composition of the rest of the group at that particular session. As not all parents were able to attend all workshops, this meant that changes in thinking seemed more tentative than in Wood Close Primary School.

Parent-Led Workshops: The Importance of Relationships

In order to inform and enthuse parents about the workshops, Ben (who was a full-time researcher on the project) spent a lot of time prior to the introductory sessions chatting to parents in the school playground about the project when they had just dropped their child off or were waiting to pick them up. We also distributed flyers with photographs of us, as the project team, that explained who we were and what the project was about. This kind of activity was crucial to the success of the project: it helped parents become familiar and comfortable with who we were and what we were doing, and we hoped it made us seem less intimidating. This type of time investment is seldom built into research or intervention projects but is necessary to help develop relationships with parents so we could support their confidence in attending the workshops and sharing their thinking and experiences with us. This was particularly important for parents who may not be used to spending time in school beyond drop-off and pick-up times. By the introductory workshop session, then, we had already started to build relationships with parents (and with schools, as hosts) through the focus groups, through hanging around in the playground and through giving out introductory flyers.

Once the workshops had started, it was important for our approach that they would be led by parents: we were aiming to empower parents and felt that part of this was foregrounding parents' expertise and supporting them to recognise that they already knew a lot more than they thought they did. In practice, however, this dynamic was very challenging to maintain. We aimed to position ourselves as workshop facilitators rather than workshop leaders. This started with us dressing casually: jeans and jumpers, rather than more formal, smart attire. This was picked up on by some parents, who said that they felt comfortable talking with us as we were 'wearing cosy jumpers and didn't look scary'. There were other factors that were harder to control, however.

The workshops were taking place in a school, and we had come from the university – and this led to some parents assuming or expecting that we would be acting as teachers in a directive role. In the workshops, some parents looked to us to give them examples of everyday activity that they could say they had or had not done, they looked to us to give them examples of what their thought processes might be in different activities, and to name the maths that was inherent in such activity. They looked to us for confirmation that what they were saying was correct. This was perhaps unsurprising, as it was consistent with expectations (and anxieties) around mathematics in school: it was viewed by parents as a distinct curricular subject, and interactions were expected to echo those in school with us as teachers and parents as pupils. To move out of this dynamic required a great deal of inhibition on our part. While it would have been easy for us to give our own examples of everyday activity and the mathematical thinking within that activity, it was important not to tell the parents what to think. We also wanted, to some extent, to model the kinds of interactions that we hoped parents would have with their children – conversations where ideas are being explored together, rather than one person telling another what they should know or think. But when we were sitting there with several parents looking at us and apparently waiting for us to tell them what we thought they should know, it was very challenging to remain quiet and not lead the conversation: we wanted to step away from a teacher-led model. We were trying to be 'not school-like' in terms of the content of what we were discussing and how we were hoping parents would interact with their children, so we needed to support this with our actions and interactions as well.

The roles of the different facilitators also helped us in developing a parent-led dynamic. Tim (who was also a parent) and Jo (who was not a parent) were both confident in mathematics, but Ben (also a parent) was not at all confident in maths and viewed himself as 'not a maths person'. Ben attended all the workshops, while Tim attended the workshops at Crossways and Riverside Primary Schools and Jo attended the workshops at Wood Close and Queen Street Primary Schools. Ben's initial lack of confidence in mathematics had some element of insiderness with the parents in our workshops – he was exploring ideas alongside them and recognising mathematics that was inherent in activity at the same time as the other parents. This modelling by one of the facilitators of process, of how we hoped parents would come to recognise their own activities, was useful in helping us step away from a more 'expert-led' mode of interaction with parents.

Focus of Workshops

The way in which the workshops developed, as we explain above, was not focussed on curriculum maths. This was contrary to the expectations of the funder, the schools and some of the parents. The further we were through the process, the more we realised this disjuncture in expectations and how important it was in the framing of the workshops. The project funder (with whom we had good communications and relationships) told us about other projects where schools supported parents with curriculum maths, and homework support, and suggested that we link up with them. Our project, however, was not directly focussed on children's attainment (although of course we hoped that would eventually be positively impacted), but was instead about family-learning conversations. As the workshops progressed, we realised that they weren't even especially about mathematics: the boundaries of the formal school curriculum weren't important. What was important was the relationship that parents had with their children and their children's learning. This focus led us to question what we were doing in the workshops and what our motivations were. This will be discussed in subsequent chapters.

Chapter 5

The Politics of Purpose

This chapter opens the second part of this book, where we examine some of the themes of the work presented in the first four chapters. Hopefully at this point, we have made a good case to the effect that children's out-of-school mathematics learning is an interesting and important focus for attention. But we also think that we have started to make the case that there is a great deal of complexity in this topic too. Our aim in this second part of the book is to engage with this complexity in some depth and to consider what might be some of the implications for theory and practice from our own research experience together with some of the research literature in this area. Readers will not be surprised to see that we do not advocate a one-size-fits-all approach, but rather one that attends, at least to some extent, to the context of individual children, families and schools.

In this chapter, we will discuss the ways in which mathematics education is constructed in terms of purpose and more specifically on the purposes that individuals have in mind when they engage in, support or encourage out-of-school mathematics learning. We suspect that a great deal of the difficulty and conflict around out-of-school learning stems from differences in the purposes that people have in mind. Conversely, we have a reason to believe that an understanding of the multiple purposes at work in this domain should lie at the heart of any effective strategy to improve learning. Mathematics education for some groups can sometimes be seen, for example, as having the purpose of getting as many children and young people as possible to achieve as well as possible in mathematics examination at school-leaving age. However, other groups may feel that mathematics education has other purposes – with as much or higher value than passing exams. We will explore some potential purposes that groups may have in mind as we go through this chapter.

Implicit in the last paragraph is the idea that as well as asking 'what' are the purposes of mathematics education, it will be important to ask 'for whom' are they important (Biesta, 2009; Bogotch et al., 2007). There are myriad stakeholders in mathematics education, including children and young people, the parents of those children and young people, teachers and school leaders, subject associations and other groups concerned with informing policy and practice relating to mathematics education, and national and international governmental organisations.

Parental Engagement and Out-of-School Mathematics Learning, 49–61
Copyright © 2023 Tim Jay and Jo Rose
Published under exclusive licence by Emerald Publishing Limited
doi:10.1108/978-1-78769-705-820231005

Mathematics for Government and Schools

We use the phrase 'politics of purpose' in the title for this chapter because the negotiation of different purposes, goals and outcomes in education is inevitably political. National and school curricula and assessment frameworks set the tone for education to a large extent. On its first page, the maths curriculum for England and Wales says of mathematics that, 'It is essential to everyday life, critical to science, technology and engineering, and necessary for financial literacy and most forms of employment' (DfE, 2014). There are multiple purposes for maths teaching and learning in this one sentence, but they really group into two categories: mathematics for employment; and mathematics for everyday life. Knowledge and understanding of mathematics is certainly an important criterion for success in many jobs in science, technology and engineering. And a mathematics qualification in itself gives young people access to many forms of employment and further education. The vast majority of undergraduate courses in the United Kingdom require a minimum grade in mathematics at GCSE as part of their admissions requirements, even when there is not much mathematical content in the course (see Stevens, 2013, for a discussion of this phenomenon). Mathematics is also useful in negotiating many different aspects of everyday life. The example given in the sentence above is 'financial literacy' but one could also argue that a good level of knowledge and understanding in mathematics would support good time management and planning, navigation as well as a variety of other household tasks – estimating the amount of paint required to decorate a house, for example. There is some room for discussion around both of these purposes of mathematics teaching and learning, however, and about whether much mathematics teaching in schools has a focus on mathematics for employment and mathematics for everyday life.

There is a further purpose of mathematics teaching, alongside but also tangled up with the practicalities of preparing for life and work. Mathematics attainment functions as a kind of proxy for educational success, both inter- and intra-nationally. International comparisons in mathematics attainment, including TIMSS (Mullis et al., 2012) and PISA (Stacey, 2015), are drivers of mathematics teaching and learning in countries that participate (e.g. Oates, 2011). Within England, primary schools are ranked according to pupils' performance at age 11, with scores in reading and mathematics contributing to the measure of performance. Therefore, mathematics attainment *in itself* constitutes an important outcome of teaching and learning for some. Other writers refer to the *use value* and *exchange value* of mathematics learning and attainment (Williams & Choudry, 2016) to refer to and discuss the multiple and sometimes competing purposes of mathematics teaching in schools. Here though, it will be sufficient just to make the point that mathematics teaching in the classroom has more than one purpose and that these purposes may sometimes be in conflict with one another.

Multiple Purposes of Mathematics Education

Biesta (2009) provides a framework for thinking about the purpose of education in general but uses mathematics education as a particular example. Biesta suggests that a distinction should be made between purposes with *instrumental* value and purposes with *universal* value. Purposes with instrumental value would include the passing of exams, for individual young people, the achievement of a high placing in league tables for schools and the achievement of a high placing in Trends in International Mathematics and Science Study (TIMSS) or Program for International Student Assessment (PISA) rankings, for national governments. Biesta proposes that consideration ought to be given more often to purposes with universal value – those that may support learners towards self-actualisation.

Greer and Mukhopadhyay (2003) ask the question, 'What is Mathematics Education For?' In their essay, they suggest seven purposes of mathematics educations, which they argue are enacted to a greater or lesser extent within schools. On the one hand, they acknowledge the belief among some that the purpose of mathematics education might be to create more mathematicians. However, this view is seen as somewhat elitist, as the vast majority of those studying mathematics in schools are not destined to become professional mathematicians. A second purpose that they consider is that of preparing learners for the world of work; mathematics is seen as a vital skill for many forms of employment. Greer and Mukhopadhyay also discuss the possibility that a purpose for mathematics education is its value in helping learners to navigate everyday life, although they suggest that 'most people handle the practicalities of daily life effectively without benefit of school mathematics beyond simple arithmetic and that the knowledge and skills that are essential are acquired through learning within practices situated outside of school' (p. 4). Rather than this focus on the *utility* of mathematics for navigating everyday life, they suggest that a key purpose of mathematics education is to give learners a set of tools to analyse issues relevant to their lives and also to make sense of the world around them. This is a perspective that resonates strongly with our approach to our research projects. We have found in much of our work that there is value for children and parents just in noticing and reflecting on the mathematics in everyday life. However, we take from Greer and Mukhopadhyay the observation that there are multiple potential purposes at play where mathematics education activity is taking place, and the various participants in such activity (children, parents, teachers and researchers) may have different purposes in mind during their engagement.

Civil (2002), rather than talking about different *purposes* of mathematics education, suggests that there may be at least three different kinds of *mathematics* at play in the classroom. There is 'school mathematics', characterised by 'an overreliance on paper-and-pencil computations with little meaning, clearly formulated problems following prescribed algorithms, and a focus on symbolic manipulation deprived of meaning' (p. 41). School mathematics generally involves learners working individually, in their seats. Then there is 'mathematicians' mathematics in the school context. For Civil, mathematicians' mathematics 'deals with ill-defined problems; it requires time, persistence, and flexibility; mathematicians often refer to a certain element of playfulness in their work, of "messing around" with ideas in their search for justifications, counterexamples, and so on' (p. 42). Classrooms that focus on doing mathematics like mathematicians may involve some collaboration, some discussion and some negotiation of meanings and possible strategies. Finally, Civil's definition of 'everyday mathematics' is the activity that 'occurs mainly by apprenticeship; involves work on contextualised problems; gives control to the person working on the task (i.e., the problem solver has a certain degree of control over tasks and strategies); and often involves mathematics that is hidden – that is not the centre of attention and may actually be abandoned in the solution process' (p. 43). In a similar way to Greer and Mukhopadhyay (2003), Civil suggests that these three kinds of mathematics may often be in tension in learning situations, where different participants in a mathematics education activity may have different views on which of these three types of mathematics they are, or should be, doing.

In the data from our research projects, we have seen multiple instances of tension in participants' reports of their experience of mathematics that reflect some of the suggestions of both Greer and Mukhopadhyay (2003) and Civil (2002). Tension around these multiple potential purposes of mathematics education, and around the kinds of mathematical activity that might be at play, comes through in both children's and parents' reports of mathematics activity in and out of the classroom. Next in this chapter, we discuss some examples from the point of view of some of the children we have worked with. Then, we will discuss some examples from parents.

Mathematics for Children and Young People

Some of the first conversations that we had when starting work on these projects started with a short question for children, 'Where do you do maths outside of school?' We quickly learnt that this is not a very useful question to ask. Children reliably gave one of two answers to this question: the most common answer was that they use maths when checking change when shopping, and then the second answer was that they use maths when weighing ingredients for cooking/baking. Interestingly, follow-up questions revealed the fact that children are often not able to give many further details regarding these activities or even remember the last time that they actually did these things. Our interpretation of this phenomenon was that children were telling us about what they thought 'out-of-school maths' was, based on what they saw in maths text books and problems that they encountered in their maths classroom – they were not trying to tell us anything about their actual out-of-school experience. Thinking about this in terms of the purpose of mathematics and of mathematics education, we might conclude that from children's point of view, the main purpose is to complete tasks set by teachers in maths classrooms and to pass tests and exams in mathematics. We had to work quite hard to encourage children to explore ways that they used mathematical thinking outside of the classroom or to consider other possible uses of maths. However, we wanted to know more. We wanted to know more about why children struggle to see mathematics in their lives and activity outside of school, and we wanted to know more about how we might encourage children to make some connections between classroom maths and out-of-school activity.

One of the issues that has emerged from our conversations with children and young people has been a tension between the kind of mathematics that they experience in the classroom and the kinds of mathematics that they think might be useful for them once they leave school. When we spoke to some Year 9 students (13–14 years old and selected by their teacher as being relatively high-achieving in mathematics) during the Economic Activity and Mathematics Learning project (Chapter 3), we asked them how much they thought the mathematics they were learning in school was connected with the maths they felt they experienced or needed in everyday life. Their response was that they felt that their mathematics education to that point had not prepared them for many of the activities that one might expect that it should have. These young people mentioned things like budget planning, choosing utilities providers and making decisions about credit cards and mobile phone contracts. On the one hand, it was good to hear that the students could see that value of mathematics for helping make financial decisions. However, on the other hand it was disappointing that they did not feel like their education so far had given them the skills or the confidence that they thought they needed.

As well as having concerns about their lack of preparedness for future decisions, we also saw some tensions between classroom mathematics and contemporary out-of-school problem-solving and decision-making. We recorded some examples of these 13–14-year-old young people's experiences of mathematical thinking outside of schools – one account was particularly illustrative of a disconnect between the mathematics of the classroom and the use of mathematical thinking in the world. A group of boys were talking about things that they spent their money on and how they made decisions about what was good value for money and what was not. One of the boys told us about buying video games. He said that there were two places that he went where he might buy a new video game: a specialist video game store and a large local supermarket. He told us that he would buy from the video game store, even though the games were more expensive. Bearing in mind the fact that the exact same games were for sale in both places, to explain this decision he said that he knew there was a connection between price and quality and so he believed that the CDs for the games at the specialist store were thicker and so would be more durable and last longer. This young person was trying to make sense of price differences and of connections between price and quality, but was ultimately making decisions that were less than optimal. Now of course the mathematics involved in this kind of decision is not complicated; what may be preventing this young person from making a good decision is a mismatch between the mathematics of the classroom (linear relationships; simple and rational systems) and the structures of economic life relevant to this situation (complex systems of supply and demand; economies of scale). This example is representative of the issue that the young people raised as a group – that they are well prepared for mathematics tests and classroom activity (these pupils were high achievers in mathematics) but felt (and showed themselves to be) unprepared to translate these skills and use them to make good decision outside of school. If we extrapolate from this example of choosing among retailers when buying a video game, to situations where young people will need to negotiate and manage household economies and interact with and choose between various financial services, then we see that there is a great potential for better connections between the classroom and the mathematics of everyday life.

So we see that within the mathematics classroom, not all purposes are borne in mind equally. Of course there are reasons for this. There is no time in the school year to do everything perfectly, and so decisions must be made about what to spend more or less time on. And schools are not judged on students' ability to manage their finances once they leave. The students' complaint does draw our attention to an important issue, though, connected with the role of context in mathematics learning. It is well known that it can be very challenging for learners to transfer knowledge and understanding from one context to another (Greeno, 1997). There is a limit to the support that can be given to students in applying their mathematical knowledge and understanding to problems in the range of contexts that they may encounter beyond the classroom. Perhaps it is unrealistic for those Year 9 boys to expect their mathematics teachers to help them develop their financial literacy as well as their mathematical understanding?

In our research with younger children, we had the opportunity to explore in further detail the division in children's minds between the mathematics encountered in the classroom and the mathematical thinking that is integrated in out-of-school activity. As described in Chapter 3, we used a combination of methods, including structured diaries, photo elicitation and small group interviews with children aged 7–11-years old, to collect data on children's uses of mathematical thinking in their out-of-school lives. Several features and themes in the data revealed how children viewed the application of mathematical thinking out of school very differently to the way that they viewed classroom mathematics. We focus on two key issues here – one of these is way that children define the focus of the activity, and another is in the way that children use language to describe the nature of the activity. With respect to the focus of the activity, a key feature of the data was the fact that children *never* referred to anything they did outside of school as 'mathematical', or maths-related. They would only ever use 'maths' and related words to describe what happened during mathematics lessons in school. This is consistent with research looking at the *perceived utility* of mathematics among young children. For example, Metzger et al. (2019) found that children do not generally see any utility of mathematics outside the maths classroom.

In relation to other examples of financial literacy, in the Economic Activity project, we found that children from more middle-class backgrounds were confident to explore new activities and experiment with ideas. For example, some engaged in investments such as buying and selling model cars on Ebay or running small businesses such as jewellery-making. These children were happy to take risks, and try things out, because they could afford to fail and lose their investment. Further, these children were often more familiar with costs associated with household management. Children from more disadvantaged backgrounds, however, were less likely to entertain the risk of losing money by trying out new initiatives, and tended to use money in ways that they were familiar with, such as buying items. In short, children from middle-class backgrounds are already doing things at home that are valued by the education system, and preparing for progression in adulthood. Children from more disadvantaged backgrounds are less likely to participate in such activities, but schools can often appear to do little to support this kind of development.

We see some of these same issues around making connections between classroom mathematics and the *use* of mathematics that we see outside of school *within* school classrooms. We have visited several primary schools, for example, where mathematics is taught differently to other subjects in a way that can make it difficult for children to make meaningful connections between what they are learning about mathematics and what they are learning elsewhere. For example, children may work in different groups for mathematics than they do for other subjects because of a perceived view on the part of teachers that mathematics is better taught with children grouped by achievement. Or, while other curriculum subjects are taught in relation to a half-termly topic focus, mathematics is always taught in isolation because of its perceived abstraction from other topics (in one school we visited, all other curriculum subject were being taught through a focus on 'the rainforest', for example – but mathematics alone was being taught outside of this topic focus, with different exercise books and in different groupings).

Parents' Aims in Engaging With Mathematics Learning: Do Parents Think They Need to Be Teachers?

As part of the Everyday Maths project that we described in Chapter 4, we carried out a set of group interviews with parents of Year 3 children in primary schools. A good deal of the discussions in these sessions focussed on parents' experiences supporting their children's mathematics learning. Here, we share some of the reasons that parents gave to explain why they did not do more mathematics with their children. Later in this section, we also discuss some of the strategies that parents employed in order to try and support their children's learning in spite of the difficulties that they experienced.

Throughout the group interviews, parents discussed their involvement in their children's learning in terms of ways that they could reinforce or rehearse the kinds of teaching and learning activities that they perceived to be happening in their children's classrooms. Towards the end of each interview, we moved the conversation on to discussion of other, non-school-centred, forms of engagement with mathematics. However, all parents' initial responses to our questions about their support of their children's mathematics learning focussed on ways that they worked with school maths tasks. These were either mathematics tasks actually sent home by teachers as compulsory or optional homework or tasks from other sources designed to align with or support classroom learning – for example, revision books from publishers or websites designed to support children's classroom learning.

The focus groups showed us that while parents consider their role in supporting their child's learning to reinforce and rehearse the work of the classroom, then there are limits to the extent to which this support can be given effectively. On the surface of things, it seems that if parents' goals and purposes are aligned closely with teachers' purposes then things should work well. This is certainly the approach that schools generally seem to take – to encourage parents to rehearse tasks from the classroom at home. However, our research, backed up by previous research in this area, shows that this alignment is not always successful in supporting children's learning.

Parents have limited time to spend with children. The majority of parents in our own research, and generally in the literature on parental engagement, report that the main reason for not doing more is a lack of time. In many families both parents work full time which, alongside time required to manage a household, limits the amount of time that families have to spend together. The literature concerning parenting time is interesting – large-scale analyses of time diaries have shown that between the mid-1960s and late 1990s, parenting time across a range of industrialised countries actually increased (Gauthier et al., 2004; Sayer et al., 2004). In the United Kingdom in 1961, mothers spent an average 0.7 hours per day on childcare activity, and fathers spent an average 0.2 hours per day, while by 1999 these figures had risen to 1.7 hours per day for mothers and 0.8 hours per day for fathers (Fisher et al., 1999). We have not been able to find reliable figures since 1999 for the United Kingdom, but there is no reason to assume that time available for parenting has reduced over the last 20 years. However, these figures (1.7 hours per day for mothers and 0.8 hours per day for fathers) are still low, given that there are things other than mathematics that families will want and need to spend their time on! The mean figures are also likely to be hiding substantial levels of variance among families.

Alongside feeling that they do not have enough time to engage with children's learning as much as they might like, parents also often feel that they do not have sufficient knowledge to support their children. There is evidence of a decline in the numeracy skills of adults in England, and this appears to be accompanied by a generalised attitude of 'I just can't do maths' (BIS, 2011; NIACE, 2011). This negative attitude has been highlighted as a major obstacle for parental involvement (Williams, 2008). In a survey commissioned by the Department for Education and Skills in the United Kingdom (Peters et al., 2008), two-thirds of parents said they would like to be more involved in their children's school life. This same survey also reported a decrease over time in the confidence of parents to help their children. Peters et al. report a number of issues that can potentially undermine parents' confidence with regard to children's mathematics learning, including differences between school instruction and parents' own mathematical knowledge, parents' attitudes and anxiety towards mathematics, and parents' beliefs about their interaction with the school. Parents' misunderstanding of what their children do and the differences between the current teaching methods and their own experiences were the main reasons for lacking confidence to help with homework. Discrepancies with school-like forms of mathematics might be a consequence of factors such as cultural differences or historical changes. Parents may conceal their ways of doing mathematics from their children so they can learn schools' methods (de Abreu & Cline, 2005), and some can feel excluded from helping their children because they fail to understand newer approaches to teaching mathematics (McMullen & de Abreu, 2011).

In our own research, we saw some evidence of parents lacking mathematical knowledge, but in our group interviews, it was more common to hear parents talking about a lack of *pedagogical* knowledge or about their unfamiliarity with the way in which schools taught maths. One parent told us:

> [. . .] my daughter comes home - she's in a support group and she comes home with these bits of paper and I look at it and I go. . . I know the answer, it's very simple, I can't see this explanation of how you've got to work it out, how on earth does that work? And that's where I find myself getting lost.

Here we see a mathematically-able parent who understood the mathematics involved in a task sent home from school but did not have a sense of how to teach the content to their children. This resonated with comments from a substantial number of other parents in our sample. While a simple lack of mathematical knowledge is theoretically manageable through tuition for parents, this phenomenon of knowing the mathematics but not understanding the particular procedures or teaching approach being used in the classroom is less easy to remediate. As discussed above, workshops run by the school can work in the short term for specific aspects of the curriculum, but cannot cover the full range of mathematics that children will be learning. This means that there will always be a risk that parents have a lack of confidence in supporting children with mathematics tasks that come home from school.

In one school, we spoke to a group of eight parents from a school with a relatively more middle-class demographic than others we worked with. During this session there was a long discussion about the information that parents received from their school about their children's learning. These parents felt a very strong sense of responsibility to help their children with the mathematics that they were learning at school. They told us that when their children had been in the infant school (Reception to Year 2, between 4 and 7 years of age), they had received quite a lot of information about the work that their children were doing. For example, a whiteboard outside the school entrance would show that week's learning objectives. Now that their children were in year 3, and had moved to the junior school, parents felt they had much less information about what their children were learning.

The reason that the amount of information was felt to be important was very strongly connected to parents' perception that they were insufficiently equipped to support their children's learning. One mother told us:

> And you need it at the beginning of the week I think because, like, I'm the same, I take – if I get a chance I'll take a photograph of this thing, it's just a whiteboard (but if I get a chance to look at it. . . whether we do it's a different matter), but at least you've got something.

This mother felt she needed to know all of the week's learning objectives before they were taught to children. Two reasons were given for this. The first was that it would give parents time to do some research about the topics so that they were better prepared to help when children needed it. The second reason was that parents could do some work with children to help prepare them for what they were going to be doing in class. Many parents that we spoke to told us the same thing, that they wanted to feel much better informed about what was happening daily in the mathematics classroom, so that they would feel better able to support their children's learning at home. Of course, there is a line in the quotation above, 'if I get a chance to look at it... whether we do it's a different matter', that points to the limited amount of time that parents have available to engage with school-centred mathematics tasks. We must also face the issue that what parents are asking for may not be as possible or indeed as helpful as they think it would be. As an example of this, there were a number of conversations, during the focus group interview sessions, regarding workshops that were provided by schools in order to help parents understand some of the mathematics that children were learning. While parents reported finding these workshops helpful, they also recognised the fact that they were not sustainable in the long term as a means of keeping up with what their children were learning in the classroom. The content of workshops often involved work on arithmetic methods (using the 'chunking' method for division, for example) so that parents could support practice at home. However, once children had mastered the particular skills covered in the workshop, or the classroom had moved on to a new area of the curriculum, then parents found themselves in need of further information. They recognised that it was not possible for a set of workshops to give them all the knowledge that would be required in order to support children's learning across the whole curriculum. Some parents went further than participation in school workshops to try and keep up with their children's learning. A group of parents in one school told us that they were enrolled in their own mathematics classes. They said that their main motivation for taking part in these classes was to be better able to support their children with their own learning. One parent was studying towards an Entry Level 2 qualification in mathematics (around the level expected of a 7–9-year-old child in school in England). This parent was clearly making an enormous commitment and investment of time and other resources in order to study mathematics and to develop her confidence in supporting her child. But she too reported that she felt that it was very difficult to 'keep up' with her child's progress in the classroom, and was not confident that she could learn quickly enough to be able to effectively support her child's learning at home.

Effective Partnership

Much of this chapter has focussed on ways in which purposes of different groups do not align. We have seen that parents' perceptions are often out of alignment with teachers', and that children and young people feel that mathematics lessons in school are not adequately preparing them for life and work. Furthermore, there is a wide range of variation among families with regard to social, cultural and mathematical capital, and among schools in terms of overarching attitudes to home–school communication and to parents. Here we consider how these issues can be addressed, primarily by recognising these different purposes and motivations and by exploring ways to allow them all to be actioned and valued.

We have seen in some of the examples of parents' reports on their experience of supporting mathematics learning at home that there is great potential for conflict. We have also seen that many common practices, including practices around homework and home–school communication, can exacerbate conflict in different ways. In line with the title of this chapter, we have suggested that some conflict can be interpreted in terms of misalignment of purpose.

The core of the problem consists in the fact that parents can never fully align with schools' mission to raise attainment in national standardised tests. Please note that this is not to say that this is all schools' exclusive mission; of course, we recognise that schools have other ambitions in mind for children alongside performance in tests. However, attainment in tests – especially in mathematics and English – is a key performance indicator for schools in the United Kingdom and so is an important focus of their work. We also do not mean to say that outcomes of national standardised tests are not important for parents – parents know that doing well in such tests is likely to be associated with benefits for their children in a number of ways. What we are referring to is the fact that the work required to directly improve children's attainment in standardised tests is quite a specific endeavour, requiring a specialised set of skills and knowledge. For example, a very large amount of technological knowledge is required, to understand the curriculum content, the demands of the tests and the ways that children will need to respond to questions on the test in order to achieve a good score. This is alongside knowledge about the mathematics itself, knowledge about how children learn and pedagogical knowledge about how mathematics can be taught. This is the knowledge that teachers have and parents do not. When parents told us in interviews, as discussed above, that they thought their role was to replicate and to reinforce at home the learning that children were experiencing in their classrooms, we also saw immediately parents' concerns that they did not have the information and experience that they needed to actually do this effectively.

The Everyday Maths workshops provided a prompt for parents to shift their thinking about the purpose of mathematical activity at home in three key ways. The first way in which we encouraged parents to shift their thinking was to encourage them to position themselves as experts. We did this by setting the focus of conversations on the nature and dynamics of family activity, rather than on the mathematics. This opened up opportunities for conversation that had been closed before – parents felt freer to start a conversation about some aspects of family play and activity that might go on to have some mathematical content than they had done to start a conversation specifically about mathematics. A large part of this freedom and comfort consisted in the confidence that comes with expertise. The second way in which parents were encouraged to shift their thinking was to replace the goal of 'reaching objectives' with a goal of 'creating opportunities'. As an example of the 'reaching objectives' mindset, here is an extract of data from an early workshop with parents:

> No, on the rope swing...I had a little chat about why you swing and how fast should you swing and the idea that, in theory, you should swing to the same height on the other side. It's always difficult, that, because of course in practice you don't get...you let the rope go on its own, it doesn't go anywhere near, which is always a bit tricky. But, yeah, I couldn't get much more out of that.

In this extract we see a parent talking about a conversation that they had started with their child with a clear intention of trying to impart some knowledge about pendulums. However, because the parent's understanding of the knowledge they were trying to share with their child was half-remembered and incomplete, this proved difficult, and the parent perceived the interaction to be something of a failure. In contrast to this, we see a parent in a later workshop noting that, 'It's about knowing the right questions to ask rather than the right things to say. Where the goal is been by parents as being to facilitate conversation and reflection on things that the child cares about – in a way that might potentially bring about some mathematical thinking and learning – then interaction becomes easier and more fruitful for both parent and child.

Finally, an overarching way in which we encouraged parents to shift their thinking was to consciously 'lower the stakes' of mathematical activity outside of school. Both of the previous points fed into this – the stakes were lowered by both keeping the focus on shared reflection on play and activity, and by aiming to create opportunities rather than reach a goal in a conversation. However, the idea of 'lowering the stakes' appears to be a useful reminder for parents that encourages shared reflection and the emergence of mathematical thinking from play and family activity.

Trust

For effective home–school partnership and parental engagement in children's learning, there must be some development of trust between practitioners and families. At the most basic level, practitioners and families need to be able to trust one another that both have children's best interests at heart. This seems like it should be taken for granted, but conversations with both parents and teachers during the project showed us that this is often not the case. The problem of lack of trust revealed itself in comments that were more or less subtle – ranging from 'I know that they have a class of thirty to look after' from a parent, implying that they couldn't expect their children to receive very much individual attention, through to 'our parents are a bit rubbish', from a teacher who felt that parents of children in her school were not willing or able to support their children's education.

We argue that this conflict and lack of trust results at least in part from different understandings of the purposes of education. What we have done in our research is to work with parents and teachers to broaden understandings of the purpose of education – including by raising the profile of 'everyday maths' as an important part of children's mathematics learning. Parents are in a position to support children's mathematics learning at home in a way that teachers cannot in the classroom. Some aspects of mathematical thinking and learning highlighted at the beginning of this chapter, including Civil's (2002) 'everyday mathematics' and Greer and Mukhopadhyay's (2003) reflection on and analysis of the mathematics of everyday life and interactions, are arguably easier to support outside of school for a parent who can give their full attention to one child and their experiences, compared with a teacher in a classroom managing 30 different sets of interests and understandings. We feel that there is space for many schools to progress home–school relationships by promoting this kind of division of labour where classroom learning and out-of-school learning are seen as complementary rather than additive or oppositional.

We see the potential for tension in this comment from a parent:

> Okay. So one of the problems is that at school they're mostly concerned with. . . multiplication and arithmetic rather than all this otherstuff [Everyday Maths] which, admittedly, is maths. So then, I guess the problem is, I'm always thinking, "Well, how am I going to reinforce the stuff they're doing at school? How do I make that relevant, because actually it's not?". . .So it's almost like you're arguing for a different maths course right at that point. You wish the children did the maths that was relevant to the world rather than trying to make the world relevant to the maths they're doing [in school].

What we observed through the Everyday Maths workshops was many parents reconciling this tension by recognising that both 'School maths' and 'Everyday maths' were helpful ways for children to experience mathematical thinking and learning, and that actually they were complementary to one another rather than in opposition.

Chapter 6

Methods of Engagement

This chapter will explore the methods that we used to engage children and parents in our research, and to encourage schools (who acted as gatekeepers) to support us in our endeavour. Both the Economic Activity project and the Everyday Maths project demonstrated that children and families use a wide range of mathematics in their everyday lives. Integrating this into mathematics teaching in the classroom is complex in many ways, however, as we explored in Chapter 5. In part, this complexity arises from the way in which mathematics is taught and discussed in schools. It also stems from the wide variation of ways in which mathematics is used in family life. Exploring this variation presents interesting methodological challenges. Because we were interested in spontaneous activity and conversation, it was not feasible for us to gain an understanding of mathematics in different families' lives through direct observation. For this to work, there were several steps that we needed to achieve.

Firstly, we needed to be able to access children and parents, to enable us to recruit them to take part in the project. In both projects, we worked with schools to recruit participants: they provided access to large numbers of potential participants of the age groups we were interested in. Once we were discussing the projects with our potential participants, we needed to present the projects to them in ways that would make them want to participate and demonstrate the potential benefits of taking part. Once participants were working with us, we needed children and parents to be aware of the kinds of activities we were interested in, to remember examples of such activities in between our meetings with them and be happy to share those examples with us. Both the Economic Activity project and the Everyday Maths project, then, required interest and an investment of time and intellectual engagement from our participants that would be sustained over the duration of the projects.

Participation in both our projects involved much more than just responding to surveys or interviews or participating in other one-off activities – both projects incorporated a slightly longitudinal element, whereby each activity built on the previous one. The Economic Activity project entailed school pupils in Years 6 and 9 recording aspects of their everyday lives and discussing them in class. The project had several stages, two of which required children to work independently from the researchers to collect examples of activity and ideas from their everyday

Parental Engagement and Out-of-School Mathematics Learning, 63–73
Copyright © 2023 Tim Jay and Jo Rose
Published under exclusive licence by Emerald Publishing Limited
doi:10.1108/978-1-78769-705-820231006

lives (in diaries and through photographs). This recording of activity and ideas needed to happen without the researchers there to prompt or guide participants through the process, and the examples would be shared with researchers and other participants at a later date. In the Everyday Maths project, we started with surveys and focus groups with parents. In four schools we then progressed onto a series of monthly workshops where parents had ongoing conversations and discussions with each other, with the researchers, about family activity, mathematical thinking, and with their children.

Engaging With Schools

We used schools as venues to meet and work with participants during both of these projects. Given the focus of the research on out-of-school activity and learning, this brings to the fore a curious dichotomy of perspectives: the school's focus on curriculum-driven content and our focus on informal learner activity. The associated implications of this are discussed in other chapters. In our planning (especially for the Everyday Maths project), we considered whether it would be appropriate to conduct the research in schools. One of the key advantages of schools is that they can provide ready access to participants. In the Economic Activity project our research activity was with children. In the school setting, there are large groups of children within specific age groups, who are all there at particular times and all covering the same kind of content in their school maths lessons. Additionally, schools can facilitate access to children's parents for purposes of consent to participate in the research. So even though we were interested in children's out-of-school activity, it made sense to recruit children through schools and engage schools in the research process, as gatekeepers at the very least. In the Everyday Maths project, we worked with parents. Again, schools provide an access point to several parents of children within particular age groups. Schools also provide a venue in which to conduct the research, with space and in a location that people know.

In the Economic Activity project, participants were easy to access once the school had agreed to take part. Children were present in the classroom when we introduced the project, and they appeared to see the activity as an interesting and engaging welcome break from more regular day-to-day school work. Participants remained enthusiastic through the process – perhaps because they were sharing what went on in their home lives, which is somewhat unusual in the classroom context. In the Everyday Maths project, schools acted as gatekeepers, but parents still had to consciously and voluntarily make the effort to turn up and join the workshops – and of course be available when we were running the workshops. For the project to work, we needed ongoing enthusiasm and availability from our parent participants. Both projects, then, required schools to be willing for us to use their premises as a site for our research, and by implication they needed to be willing to be associated with the projects. Once schools had come on board, we also needed participants to be willing and able to take part and (importantly) to continue to take part.

Schools, then, acted as gatekeepers for participant access and, once the projects had started, as supporters and facilitators of the projects through their communication with participants and providers of resource. Additionally, their support for the projects either implicitly or explicitly sent the message to participants that they believed our research was important. As with any research project that takes place in schools, this meant that our relationships with schools were as important as our relationship with participants (Goff, 2020).

So why were schools willing to participate in our projects? Pupil attainment in mathematics is important for schools (as discussed in Chapter 5), and it may be that schools were keen to be involved in anything that might help. Because we weren't sure exactly how our projects would play out over time, however, and what impact they would have on participants, we couldn't use this to persuade schools to participate. We explained to schools why we believed what we were doing was important and schools bought into that, but we could not promise improved pupil outcomes and school performance. It is possible that schools were also attracted by our engagement with parents – this is something that schools recognise the importance of but have historically found difficult (Hornby & Lafaele, 2011). In the Everyday Maths project, our work with parents may have helped break down some barriers that schools experience in parental engagement.

Despite schools' willingness to participate in the Everyday Maths project, their involvement was limited and often the schools did not seem especially interested. We worked with parents, not directly with the children, and our project did not seem to intrude on the school day. As researchers, we developed relationships with the office staff who we saw when we set up the workshops and who helped us with logistics, and occasionally we discussed the project with a member of the Senior Leadership Team. This again demonstrated the low-stakes nature of what we were doing. While schools helped in terms of access to parents so we could encourage them to participate, much of the relationship-building was done informally by us with parents in the playground. Once schools in the Everyday Maths project had allowed us access, their involvement was fairly minimal and we had to focus on engaging the parents.

Enthusing Our Participants

In the Economic Activity project, when schools had agreed to take part in the project, our participants (school pupils) were easy to access. We worked with class teachers, in class time, and project activity was positioned as school work. The teacher introduced the researchers to pupils and the research activity was presented as class exercises. For the project to succeed, however, we still needed pupils to be enthusiastic and motivated – there were activities for them to complete outside of school when they were at home. The importance of us being able to access the classroom in the first place, however, cannot be underestimated. This situation raised the issue of ongoing consent. From a research ethics perspective, the usual approach is that participants should be able to decline to participate in the project if they felt like it, or to stop participating after they had started. Here, though, the school was acting as a gatekeeper and – as part of positioning our project as a classroom teaching/learning activity – the school required the pupils to participate. Teachers decided that the project was 'a good thing' and worked with researchers to implement the activity.

So how did we negotiate this tension between genuine consent and the research being positioned as classroom learning which is something that children generally cannot opt out of? Participants and parents were able to opt out of us using the children's work as data for the research – but no one actually did opt out. It is hard to say whether this is because no one wanted to, or because they felt they couldn't. When researching with children in any context – perhaps even more so in schools because of those expectations about adult/child relationship dynamics – it is important to read non-verbal cues and to be attentive to signs of discomfort or reluctance (Bourke & Loveridge, 2014). In the Economic Activity project, we reflected on children's enthusiasm for the project. This was class activity, but the nature of it was different from many class activities they might otherwise do. The children used cameras, and they discussed their home life in class: this was seen by many as a fun and exciting change and the children were enthusiastic in their participation.

With the project being situated in school, the concept of opting out is perhaps difficult for pupils to contemplate, even if the separation between activity and data is clear. Opting out is not something you can usually do in school. By constructing the project activities as something that we hoped would be fun and engaging for children, we hoped that they would want to participate and stay engaged. Research participation should be seen as something that is engaging and enjoyable – fun rather than obligation (Bourke & Loveridge, 2014). It is important to reflect on whether participants focussing on the process of participation, and not seeing the end result of the research as important enough for them to worry about, is ethically appropriate. We should of course make it clear to participants what a research project is about, what will happen to data we collect and so on – and this should be done in terms that participants can understand – but the fact remains that many participants seem unconcerned about what we then go on to do with the data. Does this matter? There are likely to be consequences of participating that are not connected to the ultimate aims of the research: enjoyment is of course one of these, and maybe also prompting wider reflection on everyday activity, what participants do and know. Whether the children had an interest in the research outcomes that do not directly impact on them personally is harder to understand, perhaps even more so because the concept of research is so far outside of children's usual frame of reference.

Motivating parents to participate in the Everyday Maths project presented a different set of questions for us to negotiate as researchers. Unlike children in a classroom, there are few times and places where we could be sure that several parents would be available on a regular basis. We used schools as a base for the workshops, but we needed to enthuse and engage individual parents so they would join the sessions and hold the sessions at a time that would work for parents. Decisions about what time of day to hold the Everyday Maths workshops were made following discussions with parents in each of the schools. In most schools we ran the workshops around 9 a.m., after parents dropped their children off. This had the advantage of parents already being on site, and not having to make a special journey in, but of course meant that we were not able to work with parents who had full-time jobs, and it didn't always fit in with those parents on shift work, for example. While schools often discuss the challenges around engaging parents (Feiler, 2009), it is worth considering the different reasons for this. It is easy to position a lack of parental engagement around confidence, but for some schools (for example, in the Everyday Maths project, Crossways Primary School with a relatively middle-class intake), involvement is perhaps less predicated around confidence and more around availability. Where parents are in full-time work – whether that be salaried or hourly paid roles – they are unlikely to be able to take time out to attend a voluntary workshop. Our decisions on timing of the workshops, then, were based on a 'least worst case' scenario – no single time of day would work for all parents, and we based our decision on a combination of availability and ease for parents.

While the timing meant that parents (at least, those who had no further commitments at that time) could stay after they had dropped their children off at school, we still needed to encourage them to come into the building and join the group. The Everyday Maths workshops were essentially a short-term longitudinal intervention, where the methods developed as we progressed through the series of sessions. This meant that we had to work hard to get parents interested and involved, and to stay involved. We let parents know about the project by giving out leaflets in the school playground, we got to know parents by hanging around with them at pick-up time, chatting with them about our project and plans for the workshops, we asked parents we met in the playground to tell their friends, and we were clear that there was no obligation for them to participate. All these principles – using flyers, developing trust, snowballing and being explicit about rolling consent – are fairly straightforward, common-sense approaches to recruiting adult participants for interventions and have been highlighted as ways to engage participants from hard-to-reach populations (Berger et al., 2009). Further principles that we used, such as providing translators where needed, working hard to develop individual relationships, regular communications (in-person, and by text and email) to develop buy-in and trust, and explaining what participation involves, have also been highlighted by Ratto et al. (2017) as strategies for recruiting participants to clinical trials. Of course, our research was very different from a clinical trial – far less structured and requiring less commitment from participants for successful implementation of the research design – but the principles of encouraging and supporting participation remain.

It is possible that the low-stakes nature of our project made it feel friendlier and more accessible for participant, but it is also possible that this characteristic made us easy to ignore. We hoped our workshops would be useful for parents (and their children) in the long run, but it was unlikely that they would see an immediate, explicit, tangible, observable difference in their children's outcomes. If parents decided not to attend, there was little sense that they might lose out on something. We hope that what we were doing would influence the way parents thought about supporting their children, but ultimately we were not measuring this. For parents, our project was not something that would lead to an immediate, observable difference in their children's educational outcomes. That we were not focussing on formal outcomes might have made us more approachable, but it also removed a potential motivation for parents to participate.

Additionally, we were deliberately not telling parents what to do – we didn't have 'answers' to their questions about helping their children with maths. We were working with them to reflect on, share and discuss their everyday activity and their interactions with their children – we were facilitating the sharing and development of ideas, but we were not providing instructions for them to follow, which would lead to a clear outcome. Conducting research of this kind, in this context, is interesting: the participants who stayed with us were a particular subset of parents who were motivated, who were comfortable with uncertainty, who were happy to just try things out, and of course who had the time and headspace to engage and to stay involved. We held one workshop a month in each school, and while parents did continue to come along, in hindsight once a week or once a fortnight would likely have helped us to maintain more momentum. For us as a research team running the workshops for the first time, the time in between workshops was helpful as it enabled us to reflect on what we had done, how it had worked and what needed to be done next. But if the workshops were to be repeated, shorter intervals between each one would likely help maintain parental motivation to stay involved.

Some schools in the project positioned their parents as hard to reach and explicitly told us that they didn't expect parents to engage. Existing research on parent/school relationships explores possible reasons for why schools may find engaging with parents challenging, and critiques the deficit concept of hard-to-reach parents in education. This concept of hard-to-reach can be turned around, instead considering why schools might be hard-to-reach for parents, and why outreach by schools can be hard for parents and families to accept (e.g. Crozier & Davies, 2007; Wilson, 2020). The terms on which schools often attempt to engage parents, focussing more on formal education, and asking parents to engage in specific curriculum-focussed support are potentially problematic: given the anxiety shown by parents in the Everyday Maths workshops around the formal curriculum and the effort it took to step outside of framing learning in those terms, this seems likely.

Parental involvement in children's education and parental involvement as participants of research are two separate issues, however. Parents may feel anxious about the formality and high-stakes nature of contact with their child's school, where it is focussed on their children's educational outcomes (Goodall & Montgomery, 2014; Hornby & Blackwell, 2018). Other considerations are likely to come into play when they are trying to decide whether to participate in research. Timing of participation, clear personal or societal benefits resulting from the research, influence of peers, first impressions of researchers, and rewards and incentives have all been discussed as factors that influence participation decisions (Hughes, 1998; Lewis, 2009). In particular, where resources (such as time) are limited, it might be hard for parents to justify the time taken to participate, if they cannot see how the research will benefit them (Wilson, 2020). This is why hanging around and getting to know parents, and chatting to them about the research (as we did at the school gates) can pay dividends in recruiting parents as research participants (e.g. Crozier & Davies, 2007; Jones & Allebone, 1999): parents can then start to feel that the researcher is part of their community, and thus what they are doing has relevance to their lives. Where time is taken to develop relationships and to get to know parents, hard-to-reach (in schools' terms) does not necessarily mean hard to research (Wilson, 2020).

Participants' Expectations About the Nature of Our Research

When parents were considering taking part in the research – and subsequently when they decided to participate – we needed to be aware of their unfamiliarity with the research process and with the landscape of academic research. For people who are not regularly involved with or consuming research, the processes and activities involved in research participation can feel strange (Schlebe et al., 2015). The types of interactions involved in research are often not the kinds of interactions that take place in everyday life: interviews and focus groups, and our workshops, are similar to the kinds of conversations that might happen in everyday life but are more agenda-driven than conversations between friends, for example, and less focussed and output-oriented than might be expected in a workplace. This is perhaps especially relevant for us, given that our research took place on school premises but we wanted parents to lead the conversations and be the 'experts'. In schools, it is usual for teachers (as representatives of the school) to lead and direct activity, and those who participate in that activity are usually positioned as learners, who follow the directions of the teachers. Of course, learners are usually children, but this dynamic will also apply to parents, where the school is trying to show parents how to support their child's learning. So in our research, we were working in a place and context where parents were used to following directions given by teachers or other school representatives, yet we were asking them to take the lead instead. We were asking parents to step outside of the role dynamics that were likely to be expected in this context.

We also had to work around parents' assumptions that there were 'right' or 'wrong' ways to do things, or 'right' or 'wrong' answers to give – a phenomenon highlighted decades ago by Anyon (1980). As researchers, when we conduct research interviews we usually take pains to tell participants that we are just interested in their thoughts, and there are no right or wrong answers. In our workshops, while participants were still taking part in a directed conversation (as a research interview is), there was an implicit agenda that parents had come along to 'learn' how to support their children's maths learning. This gives a different context to a research interview, where researchers usually have an explicit agenda of understanding participants' views on a topic. For us, parents were more likely to position themselves as attending the workshop as 'learners'. Learning about something, however, especially when it takes place in a school, is more likely to align with pre-conceived ideas around how that learning happens, with interactions between 'learners' (usually children as pupils) and 'learning facilitators' (usually adults as teachers) usually being very clearly directed by the facilitator. Alongside these dynamics, learning that takes place in schools tends to be associated with evaluation: interactions do not often involve facilitators just being interested in opinions, and learners having permission to question the way things are, but instead involve facilitators judging the accuracy or progress of a learner's understanding (Schlebe et al., 2015). This resonates with our experiences, where parents looked to us to check that they were giving the correct response and were waiting for us to tell them what was right, or wrong, or give them instruction. Research activity where the researchers are just interested in participants' ideas is likely to seem strange to participants, especially where they are not familiar with the many potential purposes of research. In hindsight, this uncertainty about expectations was possibly further compounded by our calling the sessions 'workshops': perhaps the name implied that the focus was on learning, and thus (given the school context where learning is assumed to take a particular form) may have shaped expectations around the nature of interactions.

Beyond the interviews and discussions in both projects, we wanted participants to share with us the details of their everyday lives. In each project, we gave our participants digital cameras to take photographs that illustrated activities they did. The pupils in the Economic Activity project seemed to enjoy this activity (perhaps because it was so different from their normal homework), and perhaps the concept of 'Economic Activity' was exciting and special – because it was unfamiliar. These pupils did not seem self-conscious about taking and sharing their photographs – again indicating that they found the activity fun, which of course is important in research with children (Bourke & Loveridge, 2014). In the Everyday Maths project, however, fewer participants engaged in taking photos and even fewer in using notebooks to note down activities they might like to discuss. Our mistake with introducing notebooks was that it made the activity feel like formal homework: we found this out when some parents did not return, and their friends told us that they felt awkward about not having done the homework we had set. This mistake, then, appeared to reinforce the teacher/learner dynamic that we were trying so hard to avoid with our parent participants, and made some participants feel awkward for not completing the activity. We had stressed that it was voluntary – but the activity was clearly too reminiscent of school.

Photo-elicitation techniques have great potential in enabling researchers to access and discuss events and places where they wouldn't normally be able to be present. Other researchers, however, have struggled with encouraging participants to share details of their everyday lives through photos. Participants can find it strange capturing the mundane aspects of their everyday lives (Brownlie, 2019) or assume that researchers have a specific agenda and try to meet that, rather than reliably focussing on the 'everyday' aspects of their lives (Pilcher et al., 2016). In the Everyday Maths project particularly, we had the impression of a lot of family activity that used mathematics, but that some parents felt was too ordinary to share. For many of our parent participants in the Everyday Maths project, taking photos of activities they did in their everyday lives seemed somewhat puzzling or irrelevant to them, in relation to the project. Our participants knew that the Everyday Maths project was about mathematics – this was clear in our recruitment activity. This meant that parents were 'primed' to think about mathematically based activity, and as researchers we did not fully understand how to avoid this and instead 'prime' our participants to think about the 'Everyday'. Accordingly, parents often tried to take pictures that were 'about Maths', rather than 'about Everyday', and this is how they explained and discussed the photos they took. In our project, 'Everyday' was used as a description of the 'Maths', rather than as a focus in its own right. To help parents understand what we were interested in, and to feel as though they (not us) were experts, we needed to help parents see 'the Everyday' as a focus in and of itself.

Alongside the challenges of participants being content to just capture the mundane, Pilcher et al. (2016) also found that participants wanted to produce a 'nice' image. The purpose of taking a photo is traditionally about creating visually pleasing image. We wanted participants to take photographs to share with us 'the Everyday' as seen through their eyes. For some, this required a code switch – a change in how participants thought about the purposes of photography. For our participants in the Economic Activity project, the younger children in Year 6 were happy to take photographs of mundane aspects of their lives and talk about it, but the photo-elicitation techniques were less successful with older children in Year 9 and of course with the adults in the Everyday Maths project. Our older participants were beginning to understand – or in the case of parents, might have already understood – the principles of photography as an art form, beyond an activity to simply record events, places or things. For the younger children, it was perhaps easier to be more direct and literal than hypothetical or metaphorical (Keil, 1986): this relates well to the use of photographs for recording everyday activity. Additionally, as their home and school lives become more separated, older children may have felt embarrassed about sharing and comparing photographs of their home lives.

The above discussion outlines some of our reflections on the process of trying to enthuse participants about our research. As our projects progressed, we also had to understand how participants responded to our methods and shape what we were doing in response to their engagement and interactions with us and with each other. In the Economic Activity project, we developed ways in which the children could share examples of their everyday activity. In the Everyday Maths project, we wanted parents to steer the direction of the project even more. We had designed the workshops to be parent-led, and while we didn't necessarily require parents to be actively engaged in the project outside of the workshops, we wanted parents to steer the direction taken within the workshops. This meant that we needed to respond flexibly to parents' conversations and participation. Where participants had taken photographs, we needed to be led by the content; where parents discussed their experiences and activities, we needed to engage with what they raised. As researchers, then, we were not in control. The shape of the workshops was not pre-defined, or predictable, and this influenced what we could communicate about what the workshops would be like and possible outcomes. This lack of clarity and structure in our ways of working further emphasised the need for parents to trust us, if we were to enthuse and motivate them to work with us over a period of time. We needed our participants to be happy to just 'try it and see what happens'.

In the Everyday Maths project, an additional layer of uncertainty was introduced by the dynamics of the individual participants involved in the workshops. Where the same group of parents attended each time, they built up a rapport with each other – and one person not coming along, or another person joining the group, could influence the comfort and ease with which the participants discussed ideas with each other. In one school, one participant seemed to draw their confidence from another specific participant. When the latter participant was not there, the former looked to us much more, as if to confirm that what he was saying was okay. It seemed here that the spark and creativity in the group dynamic was lost. In another group, in the third session a new participant attended who seemed to dominate and shut down a lot of conversation. For us as facilitators this provided a challenge – we needed to act in the moment to try to support people's confidence and to manage overbearing people – but without taking the role of teacher or leader. Bringing a group of participants together over a series of group sessions can be helpful for people to get to know each other and develop a sense of continuity (Parker & Tritter, 2006), and this resonates with our workshop experience. But we did not want to stop new people coming along, or ask people to commit in advance to coming to all the dates. As Parker and Tritter discuss, it can be challenging to keep participant groups constant – and for us, the mix of people in the session was crucial. Not only can participant familiarity support ease of interaction, but changes in group membership can also shake remaining participants' confidence that the sessions are important and worth engaging with.

Within the Everyday Maths workshops, some parents had pre-existing relationships because their children were in the same peer group. This worked to our advantage when parents could bounce off each other in the workshops, and at times made our facilitation role easier: working with a pre-established group meant that conversations required less work from us to maintain. In Crossways School, however, parents attending the workshops were confident in their role as a supportive educator of their children. They were happy to try things out, but there was a sense that they had less to gain from the workshops, and therefore less need to draw from each other to share ideas in order to develop confidence. This highlights a further way that workshops need to be responsive to parents' circumstances, interests and needs – and adds a further layer of complexity in presenting a straightforward version of how we engaged with and motivated parents to take part. Understanding parents' needs was a core part of this project: the nature of the workshops varied widely according to the group we were working with, and the interactions between the individual participants shaped the ways the workshops ran, which is reminiscent of focus group methodology (Parker & Tritter, 2006).

In summary, then, these projects required participants to be engaged and enthused by the projects, and motivated to participate. The nature and stability of the group itself meant that this motivation could fluctuate: we saw motivation growing, but we also saw parents becoming less motivated as group dynamics changed. The shape of both our projects, in terms of the ways we motivated and interacted with participants, the methods that we used to facilitate conversation and generate data, emerged over time. Our projects were not clearly defined from the start and we could not have predicted at the start of the projects what they would look like at the end. As Rose and Jay (2022) discuss, the shape of our projects developed from the ways we interacted with participants and with each other, and depended on who we were as researchers and who our participants were as individuals. Beyond communicating this uncertainty to potential participants, this also means that communicating and disseminating our research in terms of what we did and how we did it, in a way that can be replicated by others using the same principles, is potentially problematic. We had to think creatively during the project and respond using our previous research experiences, our research expertise and our understanding of it – which would be different from how someone else would respond to participants and thus how the workshops would play out over time. We cannot say that what we did was the 'best' way to achieve our aims, although it did enable us to develop our understanding of out-of-school activity.

Working to engage participants in ongoing research projects can require this kind of flexibility and entails using our relational skills to respond in different ways to different participants. For us, this applied to methods of engagement with participants, to methods of data collection and to the direction of our projects. Our projects were not participatory projects because we were still using the projects to achieve our ends as researchers – we, as researchers, 'owned' the projects and determined what each step should be – but we worked in a responsive way that was to some extent unplanned. This responsive way of working that focusses on relationships before process, letting go of control and trying things to see what works is a big step away from what we normally think of as rigour in research. It is an approach that sits in tension with traditional notions of research quality (Wilson et al., 2018). Nonetheless, paying close attention to relational dynamics in such projects has meant that there is potential for such projects to have a more profound impact on individuals involved and speak to the wider community. This speaks to Tracy's (2010) alternative notions of research quality for qualitative research. Smaller, interactive projects such as ours are often closer to what people are doing in their real lives, what people recognise and are engaged with and can see themselves doing in the future. Such work has potential for credibility and resonance, and can make a significant contribution through widespread levels of on-the-ground engagement with the outcomes of the work.

Chapter 7

The 'What' and the 'How' of Our Research: Working With Participants' Expectations

Working with participants and motivating them to stay engaged in our research inevitably involved understanding and managing their expectations about the focus of our projects. This chapter picks up from a theme raised in Chapter 6 – that of participants' understanding of the focus of our research. We will now explore the nature of the expectations that our participants held about the content and focus of our projects. Specifically, we will consider our participants' expectations about what mathematics is, about how we learn to think in mathematical ways and about the context or location (on school premises) of our project activity. We will consider how those expectations shaped the way we interacted with our participants and thus how expectations became key factors in both our methods and our findings.

Both our projects focussed on mathematical activity that occurs in everyday activity. We explored activity that took place outside of school – in the home, in families and in children's free time – to enable us to identify mathematical thinking and learning that took place in informal contexts. Over time, in the Everyday Maths project particularly, our focus became broader. As we recognised how blurred boundaries were between curriculum subjects, we focussed less on mathematics specifically and became interested in any type of conversations supporting learning that can happen in family activity. Nonetheless, our starting point was activity that involves some kind of mathematical thinking. This meant that we introduced the projects to schools and participants as being about mathematics, and schools and participants decided to become involved in our project with expectations that our research would be about mathematics learning. For children in the Economic Activity project, and parents in the Everyday Maths project, this led to preconceptions and expectations about what we as researchers were interested in. What our participants understood 'maths' to be was therefore important in shaping their expectations about what we, as researchers, wanted to understand.

Additionally, all our interactions with participants in both projects took place in schools. This was important in that it influenced the dynamics of our relationships with participants. In school classrooms, learning activity is usually

Parental Engagement and Out-of-School Mathematics Learning, 75–91
Copyright © 2023 Tim Jay and Jo Rose
Published under exclusive licence by Emerald Publishing Limited
doi:10.1108/978-1-78769-705-820231007

directed by adults who are in the teacher role. This meant that when we worked with pupils in the Economic Activity project, we were implicitly in a 'powerful' position where our participants expected us to direct activity. This issue also arose in the Everyday Maths project: parents appeared to construct an implicit learner/teacher dichotomy within our interactions, and we had to work hard to prevent ourselves being positioned as teachers in the dynamics with parents. The school context, as the location for our research projects, therefore also shaped expectations around the nature of the project and our role within that.

These expectations around content and context can be considered separately – but it was also helpful to reflect on the way they interacted. We had to manage not only expectations about what mathematics is but also be aware of the way the school context shaped those expectations of what it is and how it is taught or learnt. Given that our methods were, to some extent at least, shaped in response to initial stages of each project, those expectations played a key role in the methods we used, the data we collected and how we interpreted our findings.

Starting With Activity: Understanding the Everyday

The starting point for both the Economic Activity project and the Everyday Maths project was out-of-school activity, although we were interacting with participants within the school buildings. We wanted to understand mathematics-focussed activity and mathematics learning that take place outside of school that is not in direct response to the school curriculum. In the Economic Activity project we were interested in children's activity and learning that contained elements of mathematical thinking, and in the Everyday Maths project our focus was more on parents' perceptions and family activity that contained elements of mathematical thinking. This framing was strongly emphasised in how we presented the projects to schools and potential participants. Highlighting mathematics helped to make the projects relevant to schools' agendas and garner schools' support, which was important in terms of their role as gatekeepers. When we introduced the projects to children and to parents, to encourage them to participate, we also emphasised the focus on mathematics. We acknowledged that learning mathematics is something that people can find challenging and expressed our hope that the project would help people develop their confidence in this. Our aim was to encourage and support our participants to recognise that mathematics is inherent in their everyday activity and that they already use it in ways that they might not realise. We were not offering to teach people 'how to do mathematics', but our focus on mathematics acted as a convenient hook to attract potential participants. The subject is recognisable – we believed that people are likely to feel like they know what mathematics is, even if they are not confident in their own ability within it. This meant that participants had some idea of what they were being asked to participate in. Mathematics is also something that many people struggle with – adults (e.g. BIS, 2012; Kuckzera et al., 2016) as well as children (in 2017, for example, 25% of children in England did not reach expected standard in numeracy at age 11 (DfE, 2017).

Using mathematics as a way to attract potential participants had implications, however, for expectations around the purpose of the project and the kinds of activities that would be involved. We explicitly stated several times that we were not teaching participants how to do mathematics, and instead aimed to support them to recognise the mathematics that they already used, but perhaps did not think of as such. Participants held pre-existing beliefs about what mathematics is, what it is for and how it should be engaged with. These beliefs led to particular assumptions about how we wanted to work with them – both in terms of content and method. In our researcher roles, as we came to understand those beliefs they impacted how we shaped the projects' activities.

The Economic Activity project provided a useful learning experience for us as researchers. In the early stages of this project, we attempted to understand children's mathematical activity in their out-of-school lives. Initially, participants' thinking about where and how mathematics occurred in everyday activity seemed to be bounded by the kinds of examples often found in standard curriculum textbooks. At the start of the Economic Activity project, we found that asking children to discuss the mathematics they did outside of school resulted in a very limited range of reported activity: telling participants that we wanted to know about mathematical activity seemed to constrain their thinking. The examples they came to us with were mainly around money (especially counting out change when buying things in shops), baking (such as weighing ingredients) and time. When asked to explore these further, it became evident that our participants rarely baked and did not often count out change in shops. These activities were reminiscent of basic arithmetic examples of where mathematics occurs in everyday life, which are provided in textbooks. We believe that participants were primed to think about mathematics in terms of the school curriculum that they were familiar with, given that the projects were taking place in school. This meant that they sought out typical algebraic textbook examples of mathematical activity to tell us about. For them, mathematics was constructed as the kind of things that school textbooks described, and it appeared that our participants thought that this was the kind of activity we wanted to know about. This is why we introduced the idea of economic activity – this was a term that our pupil participants were generally not familiar with, so there were fewer expectations about what it did or did not include.

This experience helped us recognise that in the Everyday Maths project, our participants may from the start have had expectations around what mathematics is. Our first workshop with parents, then, was deliberately focussed on family activity rather than on mathematics. We explained in the first workshop that we were interested in family activity, in what parents did on a day-to-day basis with their children. As well as moving the focus away from mathematics, we also hoped that this would help to position parents as experts. We were interested in learning from them about their everyday lives, which of course they knew more than us about, and we hoped this would help us move away from the teacher/learner dynamic that we wanted to avoid.

We deliberately did not focus on mathematics in our initial conversations, to allow us to move beyond participant expectations that we wanted to hear about 'textbook examples' of everyday mathematical activity. Participants still seemed, however, primed to think about curriculum mathematics. The project was called the 'Everyday Maths' project, and participants had engaged with it because they were interested in supporting their children's mathematics learning – not because they were interested in reflecting on 'the Everyday'. The nature of what we were doing may have felt unfamiliar to parents in another way, too. Where schools send ideas for activities home, this usually involves asking parents to initiate *extra* activity, beyond that which they would ordinarily do in their everyday lives, and sometimes involving concepts they are not familiar with. With the Everyday Maths project, however, we suggest that families use the everyday activity they are already doing and are already familiar with as a starting point for conversations. The focus on the 'everyday' requires less cognitive load and less time than introducing new activity. The thought of using the 'everyday' as a tool for learning, however, clearly felt strange and unfamiliar for some parents at first.

Starting with family activity worked for some parents, but for others, it still seemed they were constrained by expectations about what mathematics was. Even during the first workshop, when we asked parents just to share the kinds of activities they had done with their children at the weekend (irrespective of whether they felt there was mathematical thinking involved or not), we found that parents often used similar examples to those used in mathematical textbooks – going shopping and working out change, baking and working out time and so on. When some parents told us about asking their children to check the change they had been given when shopping, with an impression of asking us a question about whether this was a correct answer to give, it was clear that we had not entirely succeeded in moving parents away from their assumptions that we were interested in a bounded definition of mathematics. Some participants' responses suggested that their beliefs about 'what counted' as mathematics aligned with what is often presented in textbooks as 'everyday examples of mathematics', usually illustrations of algebraic functions.

This highlighted to us that we needed to work hard to support participants to step outside their preconceptions of what mathematics is. The framing of our projects, however, which we used to give participants a sense of what they were getting involved in, and the location of our projects in schools, made it difficult to step aside from these kinds of illustrations of everyday mathematical activity that are so often used in school. Early on in the Everyday Maths project, for example, some of our participants tended to start with mathematical concepts, and search for activities that they felt illustrated those concepts, rather than starting with the activity and reflecting on the mathematics that might be inherent in that. This means that it can be difficult for children and parents to move beyond their existing mathematical understanding – if they are starting with mathematical ideas that they already know about (rather than starting with activity), then they are only able to work within their existing frame of reference of mathematics.

Starting with activity, on the other hand, gives the potential to broaden participants' perspectives of what 'counts' as mathematics. In the Economic Activity project, introducing children to the idea of 'economic activity' – a term with few, if any, preconceptions about what it involved – enabled them to step outside what they saw as the boundaries of school (or curriculum) mathematics. With parents, this was more challenging. We aimed to focus on family activity, but they knew that they were working with us on the 'Everyday Maths project', so mathematics was primed and many parents struggled to let go of this, especially at the start of the project.

The way in which participants tended to start with mathematical concepts and think about activity that fitted with those concepts was echoed in later work, when we were sharing the findings from the Everyday Maths project with teachers. We ran seminar sessions to illustrate the principles of the Everyday Maths projects and discuss with teachers how they could use the ideas from the workshops in their schools. In the seminars, we had several resources such as: toys and musical instruments; household items such as clothing, washing lines, cleaning equipment, DIY tools, kitchen equipment; maps and local information; art equipment; fabric, buttons and so on. As a starting point, we asked teachers to use these resources to help them think about their own household activities. Here, we observed teachers naming specific aspects of curriculum mathematics, then searching for resources that would help them illustrate that. Occasionally, they picked up a resource saying 'oh look, this would be great to illustrate (a specific aspect of the curriculum)'. Perhaps we should not be surprised at this: these teachers were there in their capacity as mathematics teachers, so they were primed to think about what they do in that specific role. The teachers who attended our seminars were used to designing their teaching and interactions to meet the needs of the curriculum, rather than starting with experience and seeing what learning can arise from that. Teachers with 30 children in a class, who need to meet the requirements of a national curriculum, do not have the luxury of being able to start with the activity. They need to think about what the children need to learn and construct activities to enable that to happen. Trying to extract common learning themes from the many varied out-of-school activities and experiences of 30 different children would be a large challenge indeed.

Mathematics in Context

Understanding and conceptualising mathematics as part of the context of everyday life is something to be tangled with, then. In schools, mathematics can be seen as procedural knowledge – 'techniques' that are generally taught (often in the abstract) and then applied in a specific ways to particular problems (Star, 2005). Moving beyond this procedural approach to a more conceptual way of thinking can be difficult for a number of reasons. Firstly, teachers can find it difficult to apply mathematics to real-world problems (Popovic & Lederman, 2015) although this is perhaps because starting with mathematical concepts, and trying to find real-life problems that fit those concepts, can be challenging. When this was turned around, and teachers were asked to engage in activities in a science museum and identify mathematics within those activities, application was much easier. Felton-Koestler (2017) discussed his experiences of encouraging trainee teachers to use mathematics in context. He highlighted the distinction between real-world mathematical problems that focus primarily on mathematical concepts and real-world mathematical problems that focus primarily on the real-world problems where relevant concepts are used to help pupils gain a more in-depth understanding of those problems. This is a useful distinction, which considers whether the contextualisation is used in service of understanding the mathematical concepts (as usually happens in schools) or whether the mathematical concepts are used in service of understanding the context (which is essentially the approach that we took with the Everyday Maths project). The latter, however, is potentially much more challenging for teachers to grasp, in part because of their expectations about the nature of mathematics in school. Some of the trainee teachers in Felton-Koestler's work tended to separate mathematical concepts from the context and see the 'mathematical' aspect as a separate entity that was not intertwined with the problems that the learners were trying to solve. Treating mathematics as a series of operations that is 'brought into' a context to solve a particular problem is illustrative of a conceptualisation of mathematics as a distinct and boundaried part of the curriculum.

An alternative to seeing mathematics as a distinct and boundaried subject is to consider it as a way of thinking that can be used to describe, understand and think about a problem, rather than as a series of operations or particular activities. Where mathematics is positioned as understanding a set of distinct operations, it is easy for the curricular boundaries to be reinforced. These curricular boundaries – the way mathematics is constructed and seen as a curriculum subject – can be a real barrier to recognise and discuss its use in context, as Felton-Koestler (2017) discussed. In the Everyday Maths project, this was illustrated very clearly. When parents were discussing activities they had done with their children, and ways they had tried to explore and discuss what they were doing, some were anxious about whether they were discussing mathematics, science or geography. This sits alongside our experiences with teachers in the dissemination workshops, where they tried to think of activities to illustrate particular aspects of the curriculum – essentially positioning context in service of the mathematical concepts. From this, we recognised that curricular boundaries were a potential barrier to our participants engaging with the scope and creativity of 'Everyday Maths'.

Our focus of using mathematics 'in the everyday' is similar to critical maths (e.g. Frankenstein, 2009; Turner et al., 2009), particularly in terms of the primary emphasis being on the everyday context or problem to be solved, with mathematics being positioned in service of that context or problem. A core principle of critical maths is around developing a mathematical mindset that underpins the way we think about context and problems, and potential solutions to those problems. Engaging with contexts and problems in a mathematical way and using mathematics to explore and understand a context of course provides challenges when working to a curriculum. Trying to introduce examples of mathematics in everyday context can be very challenging when there are 30 different children in a class, with 30 different sets of what 'everyday activity' looks like. Where this is attempted in text books, the examples of everyday activity that are used may not reflect the experiences of all children. Going to a supermarket, for example, may be very familiar to many children, but in today's diverse society there will be some children who have never been to a supermarket (or indeed are from homes who struggle to afford enough food). This contextual information, then, is strange and unfamiliar and immediately puts these children at a disadvantage. This is why starting with each individual's everyday activity and exploring the mathematics within that (rather than trying to find examples of everyday activity to illustrate specific mathematical problems) is potentially powerful – each individual starts with a familiar context. For teachers, however, thinking about how to bring a whole class of children together in a common curriculum by using these approaches brings real challenges.

The point of Everyday Maths, however, is that it does not work to a curriculum. Everyday Maths is about taking opportunities to explore ideas where you find them. Parents began to grasp this concept as the workshops progressed:

> I suppose it's seeing how maths naturally comes about rather than
> feeling "Right, this is a situation I've got to somehow apply maths
> to something" and just see how everyday situations brings it out.

Activity comes first, and what families do is not driven by the mathematics that might be inherent in that activity. But mathematical thinking of one kind or another is a part of much of family activity: if the activity is reflected on and engaged with using a mathematical framing, it is likely that there will be something mathematical that can be considered. The idea behind Everyday Maths is that, through highlighting the activities that families already do, and the way in which they already think mathematically – often without realising it – and making that explicit, parents will be supported to understand what they already know. Making this explicit then opens the door for family conversations around that mathematical thinking, thus supporting children's mathematical learning. This is still important and helpful, even if it does not fit neatly within curricular boundaries.

This is not to diminish the importance of the mathematical curriculum, however. Starting with context, and using mathematics in service of understanding a context or problem, can be hard to achieve if core mathematical concepts are not understood. Frankenstein (2009) considered the power that is afforded by recognising and understanding how numbers can (and cannot) illustrate and potentially solve problems, and how they can be used. Where the use of mathematics to address problems is explicitly taught in schools, the problems used are often relevant to the dominant group in society: Frankenstein uses an example of property taxes to illustrate her point. Those who are concerned with property taxes tend to be more advantaged groups in society – young people from more disadvantaged backgrounds are less likely to be familiar with, or feel the relevance of, property taxes. The problems of groups who are more disadvantaged – and perhaps therefore in most need of addressing those problems – are less likely to be used as examples of 'everyday maths'. The kind of 'everyday problems' that are used can be unfamiliar to more disadvantaged groups – who therefore also need to spend cognitive energy on understanding the problem as well as understanding the mathematics – thus disadvantaging them further when compared to their peers. This leads us back to the importance of drawing on *individual* experiences and activity to support learning, rather than making assumptions about what activities are commonplace.

Starting with relevant and engaging activity or problems as a gateway to introducing and exploring mathematics is not necessarily straightforward, however. Turner et al. (2009) discussed a mathematics club where children worked together to understand and propose solutions (drawing on mathematical expertise) to authentic local problems and issues that motivated the children – such as redesigning a local park and understanding patterns of immigration. This research drew on Gutstein's (2006) proposals that pulling together community knowledge (that values the expertise inherent in everyday lives), classical knowledge (traditional mathematical competence that is taught in schools) and critical knowledge (about the wider socio-political context) can help release the transformative power of mathematics education. In the club described by Turner et al., facilitators struggled with how best to build understanding of classical mathematical knowledge and critical knowledge. When it came to building understanding and scaffolding in mathematical thinking for problem-solving, the skills that were needed or could be used to engage with and understand a problem, could be quite complex. Learners did not necessarily have the requisite prior understanding to access ways of thinking that might be useful to meaningfully engage with a context or problem. Starting with an authentic problem has advantages in terms of relevance, but can be troublesome when the mathematics needed to address that problem is difficult or not understood. Additionally, real-life contexts that are deemed worthy of exploration are likely to have their own complexities. This is where the challenge of critical knowledge arises. Often further sets of expertise beyond mathematics were needed to understand these contexts that were shaped by political, legal, sociological, economic, geographical and cultural histories – for example, understanding patterns of immigration. In order to understand these contexts, a far wider set of expertise beyond mathematical thinking is needed.

The diverse sets of knowledge required to engage with authentic problems mean that it can be difficult to just focus on mathematical thinking (Turner et al., 2009) – mathematical understanding on its own is not enough. This explains why curriculum subject boundaries can be unhelpful in exploring authentic contexts, and why using mathematics to explore contexts and problems is not necessarily straightforward. Further, Turner et al. found that some of the children in their club were more engaged in the details of the context than in using mathematics to solve the authentic problems – for example when thinking about redesigning a local park. It was easy for mathematical aspects to become sidelined as children thought about the park, yet when discussing authentic problems it felt inappropriate to sideline the critical contextual conversations in order to just foreground mathematics. Engaging with authentic problems, then, has great potential to transform the way we think about the purposes of mathematics, but as a means to 'learn' maths is not straightforward. This again points to the role of 'Everyday Maths' as described in our research, as something to work alongside the school mathematics curriculum, rather than to replace it.

It is also important to consider that our work on Everyday Maths did not have to be about solving problems. We were encouraging parents to explore ideas and to reflect on their activity, using the mathematical understanding (or mathematical literacy) that they already had. Everyday Maths is about making explicit existing applications of understanding. As one of our participants explained, Everyday Maths can be about exploring the world together, and reflecting on why things are the way they are, how might things be different, and how we can find out about why the world is the way it is. Or Everyday Maths can be about making explicit what we already know and do, but currently do not label as mathematics – and unpicking our thinking to recognise the mathematical thinking that is quietly inherent in the way we consider the world and construct our activity.

Everyday Maths has potential to allow people to put to one side the dominant discourses of mathematics that are discussed by Frankenstein (2009). If we recognise that everyone has their own ways of using mathematics – as illustrated by Moll et al. (1992) and González et al. (2005), in their work on funds of knowledge – then this can provide a different type of power. Here, though, we come up against more complexity: recognition and understanding of mathematics are potentially rooted in societal power dynamics and norms. Those who are more skilled and confident at mathematics, and who are able to help parents recognise the Everyday Maths that they use are likely to be those who have successfully negotiated the existing societal structures and norms. As researchers, we placed ourselves in this role. Yet we have taken those structures and norms on board, and developed our own skills and understanding within that framework. We developed our expertise through our own engagement with and success in negotiating the school curriculum. That expertise is what enables us to help parents recognise the mathematics they use that does not look like the school curriculum. It is important to remember, however, that we were not setting ourselves against the curriculum: our role involved acknowledging that some people find it hard to engage with the school curriculum and offering additional (rather than alternative) approaches to engaging with mathematical thinking.

The Boundaries of the School Curriculum

In our work on the Everyday Maths project, some parents acknowledged that they found it difficult to support their children's learning solely by using the kinds of curriculum-focussed approaches and tasks that are often suggested by schools because they fit with what children are doing in the classroom. The illustrative examples of mathematics in context that are often used in schools may not be helpful for everyone (Frankenstein, 2009). Our stance was that parents already had scope within their everyday family activity to help support their children's learning, although they may not have initially realised this and it may not have been picked up by schools as illustrative of the mathematical curriculum.

The kinds of examples of mathematics in everyday lives that participants gave us in early workshops mainly involved number and arithmetic functions (adding, subtracting, multiplying and dividing). This is similar to Altay, Yalvaç, and

Yeltekin's (2017) work with young people aged around 12–13 years, who also struggled to apply mathematics to real life beyond number, shape and arithmetic. This kind of work mirrors a lot of the Key Stage 1 curriculum (DfE, 2013). However, the English National Curriculum in Mathematics at Key Stages 1 and 2 actually involves much more than this and includes, for example, geometry, measurement, sequencing, statistics and at upper Key Stage 2, ratio and proportion, and algebra. More broadly, principles of creativity can be applied to mathematical thinking, including: 'students asking their own questions; students following their own lines of enquiry; students choosing their own methods of representation; students noticing patterns; and students making predictions or conjectures' (Coles & Scott, 2015, p. 129). Nonetheless, in early workshops in the Everyday Maths project, parents did not often use these kinds of ways of thinking as examples of 'mathematical activity'. Instead, they offered numbers and arithmetic as examples, as that was what they understood to be happening in school, illustrated by this parent:

> So one of the problems is that at school they're mostly concerned with – that's unfair – but what I see is mostly a concern with multiplication and arithmetic rather than all this other stuff which, admittedly, is maths. So then I guess the problem is I'm always thinking "Well, how am I going to reinforce the stuff they're doing at school? How do I make that relevant because actually it's not?"

Through our work on both our projects, we attempted to take a broader definition of mathematics than just arithmetic and encouraged participants to discuss ideas that were more similar to the principles of creativity identified by Coles and Scott (2015). We aimed to help parents and children understand that their everyday activities – things that they were familiar with – were useful examples of mathematics in context. Families' everyday lives did not have to match the illustrative examples in text books, or conform to very narrow definitions of number and arithmetic, to still hold great value as learning opportunities.

As researchers, it is hard for us to decide how radical or otherwise this actually was. At times it feels as though we are challenging – or at least permitting people to see beyond – curricular boundaries, and that feels radical. At other times, we step back and consider that in our powerful position as the researchers leading the project, our thinking about what mathematics is and what it can be stems from those structures and boundaries that we are trying to put to one side. Both of us have experienced success at mathematics as delivered in the education system: we did not struggle with mathematical concepts when learning them at school, we are comfortable and familiar with the examples used of concepts in context. In Frankenstein's (2009) terms, we were in a powerful position with our ability to engage with the framing of mathematics that represented the dominant group in our culture. In our work, we were encouraging parents to see beyond the very structure that had enabled us to succeed, the structure that has given us the underpinning framework on which to base our understanding of mathematics.

Without that underpinning framework, would we be in a position to understand how to step around or even break down the curricular boundaries?

At times in the Everyday Maths project, it felt as though we were encouraging parents to step outside of what they imagined to be the rules of what mathematics is and how it is taught. These imagined rules included that mathematics is something where there are correct and incorrect answers to questions and that mathematics is something that is distinct from other curricular subjects:

> I don't know whether there is maths in Scrabble. I know we play Scrabble but we use a dictionary, but that is literacy or numeracy? I don't know.

However, those imagined rules tended to be ones that parents had constructed for themselves – either through their own experiences with the dominant discourses and power structures, or through their own interpretations of school-focussed communication about their children's learning. We wanted parents to recognise that these imagined rules were not necessarily helpful, and parents shouldn't feel bad for not being bound by them.

The perceived curricular boundaries of mathematics caused parents some anxiety. In our discussions with parents where they were concerned about whether they were discussing mathematics, science or geography, it became clear that parents believed that mathematics is something that is done on its own. Mathematics being distinct from other curricular subjects, then, was a perception that we framed as an imagined rule. Where mathematics is used in everyday life – that is, beyond the school curriculum – it is rarely considered in isolation. Mathematics is often used as a part of a bigger picture that brings together ideas and ways of thinking from many different 'school subjects'. As the workshops went on, parents began to become more comfortable with this:

> Yeah and you've got shape there; it links all together doesn't it? That kind of thing and putting two different dimensions together is really important because they have to do that so much. Again you've got the cross-over with science but at some point they need to understand the relationship between speed, distance, and time and the fact that volume changes in a different way than surface areas does.

and

> She was making a wand. And this friend of ours, making her a really beautiful wand with a sort of swirly thing for Christmas that he whittled himself out of a piece of beech, and she's just previously made her own much more crude using my housemate's sort of carving knife and stuff. And then so she was kind of seeing what... and then looking at the one my friend had made, and cutting the wood, filing the wood, and cutting the

wood, and all of that stuff. That's sort of DT isn't it? So it's those overlaps. And like her making clothes that's just craft – design again – and stuff. So is it that... it's that thing about maths being embedded in other subjects. It's therefore what aspect is it of those subjects?

Some of the interactions that parents described to us involved them trying to encourage their children to work out correct answers to questions they had posed (often without an underpinning structure of teaching and learning which have led to that point):

> I had a little chat about why you swing and how fast should you swing and the idea that in theory you should swing to the same height on the other side. It's always difficult that because of course in practice you don't get... you let the rope go on its own it doesn't go anywhere near, which is always a bit tricky.... And then trying to explain what the gap is, yeah. I did also try the whole... "If you stand up the top of the slope and you lift your feet why is it that it goes?" So I tried the idea that the rope is pulling you that way and your weight is pulling you that way, so the vector stuff basically.

This led us to realise that another imagined rule was the idea that mathematics was a subject where answers to questions are either correct or incorrect. This can lead to particular types of interaction which may create frustration and anxiety, when children struggle to understand or articulate the 'correct answer'. If we put to one side these imagined rules of mathematics as a distinct subject, and mathematics as something where the correct answer needs to be found, this can help to release some of the frustration and anxiety around interactions and conversations with potential for learning.

While our own understanding of mathematics gave us the confidence to step away from the school norms of how it is presented as a subject, and to encourage parents to step aside from their imagined rules, we believe that we were still holding true to the principles of mathematical thinking. We helped parents to break down the imagined rules that they had constructed in their heads to help them identify and categorise mathematical thinking. These rules have likely been constructed partly from a lack of confidence about mathematics and partly from a limited engagement with communication from schools about what is being taught in the classroom and how it is being taught. These imagined rules were used by parents as short cuts, to help them categorise their thinking as mathematical or non-mathematical – although they do not represent what we believe to be mathematics. They also seemed to place limits around parents' engagement with our framing of Everyday Maths. We realised, then, that it was important to help parents step beyond these imagined rules if they were to take fuller advantage of their existing mathematical thinking that they used in their everyday lives.

So if these rules are imagined, and mathematics is not a distinct and separate subject, and if it is not something that is defined by absolute answers to questions, what is it? Looking beyond primary school can help us reflect on this. There are some initiatives that aim to cover mathematical skills that are relevant to everyday lives (such as functional skills, core skills, financial literacy and so on) although these tend to be short-lived and not especially wide-ranging (Dalby & Noyes, 2022; Hayward & Fernandez, 2004) – mathematics for everyday life does not appear to be taken seriously. At school (and certainly in compulsory schooling), there seems little opportunity, however, to integrate mathematics with other subjects and to prepare learners for mathematically oriented careers, such as becoming engineers, statisticians, scientists and social scientists and so on. Mathematics is still presented in schools as a distinct discipline and not necessarily as part of broader interdisciplinary problem-solving. It is often discussed in terms of procedural knowledge (how you conduct operations) and conceptual knowledge (what different terms mean) (Österman & Bråting, 2019), but there is also potential to think about 'operational skill' – understanding how to apply that procedural and conceptual knowledge, and bringing those together in a real context (Österman & Bråting, 2019).

In primary mathematics, the focus on the procedural and (perhaps to a lesser extent) conceptual knowledge is perhaps even more defined. Given this, it is easy to see how parents might develop the imagined rules of mathematics that we noticed. The procedural and conceptual knowledge are still important and necessary parts of mathematical understanding which are prerequisites to application in context – but the imaginary rules seemed to put artificially tight boundaries around the nature of procedural and conceptual knowledge.

Preconceptions About How We Should Learn Mathematics

The imagined rules of mathematics that we refer to above lead to expectations about how mathematics learning should take place. The imaginary rule that mathematics has clearly delineated boundaries, where some things are clearly mathematics and others are not, links to expectations that it should be learnt as a formal, structured curriculum subject. The imagined rule that mathematics involves problems or questions to which answers are either correct or incorrect links to expectations that it should be learnt in structured, teacher-led modes, where teachers show the learner correct methods to be used in solving mathematical problems. In the Everyday Maths workshops, particularly the early sessions, participants often looked to us to confirm that what they were saying was correct. This happened even when parents were discussing family activity or the kinds of mathematics that activity made them think about. We were not discussing concepts to which there were correct (or incorrect) answers. We were discussing what families did in their time together and what parents thought about that – and as such we could only know what parents told us. Nonetheless, parents still wanted reassurance that they were giving us 'correct' answers or perhaps reassurance that what they were telling was what we wanted to know about. Nonetheless, these interactions were characterised by parents seeming to position themselves as learners and us as teachers, in an imagined mathematics classroom that operated according to the imagined rules about mathematics.

It seems, then, that mathematics as a concept has been 'schoolified' by many parents. Schoolification stems from discourses around early years education (e.g. Moss, 2013). An approach to early years mathematics education that is teacher-directed and oriented towards a formal curriculum is championed by some and is illustrated in the 'Bold Beginnings' report by Ofsted (2017). This perspective is often critiqued as being too much like school (Bradbury, 2019), hence the term schoolification. An alternative perspective to schoolification is that learning in the early years should be experiential, driven by interest and opportunities (Moss, 2008). This line of thinking points to the need for early years education to provide a range of experiences for children, in order to support learning that arises from activities that children choose to become involved in. The ways in which we were trying to encourage families to engage with everyday maths, then, present an alternative to a schoolified way of thinking about mathematics learning.

The imagined rules that mathematics is defined in its terms as a curriculum subject, and the expectations that it should be learnt in teacher-led, formal ways which lead to correct answers, mean that stepping outside schoolified ways of learning is difficult. Wider experiences beyond formal schooling, such as board games, travel, participation in sports, family outings and so on can be very useful for children in establishing a deeper understanding of context (Winter et al., 2004), but such experiences are unpredictable in terms what they look like and what the resultant learning is. This makes such experiences potentially difficult for families to initiate or manufacture with a view to facilitating specific learning. Children from middle class backgrounds are more likely to have opportunities to draw on such experiences (Jay & Rose, 2022; McNamara et al., 2020; Xolocotzin & Jay, 2020), but families from more disadvantaged backgrounds may have a more limited range of opportunity to draw on. Further, where parents have done less well in education and are perhaps less confident in their own mathematics learning – as may be the case in families from more disadvantaged backgrounds (Elliott & Bachman, 2018) – parents may be less confident in drawing out the learning potential from even everyday experience. Where parents are less confident in doing so, children have to rely on the school curriculum, and families have to rely on the school to guide them. Examples used in schools can, as we highlight above, be limited in scope and problematic for some families (Frankenstein, 2009).

For us, the location of the projects in schools and (for the Economic Activity project) the interaction between researchers and children taking place in school time meant that school was foregrounded even before we started to discuss mathematics. This primed participants to think about mathematics in schoolified ways. In the context of our projects, then, it was challenging for children and parents to step outside of their expectations around school mathematics (in terms of what it is about and how it is taught) and to trust that they would be supported to think about maths in a useful way. Further, this was difficult for us as researchers to encourage. Our aim to step outside of schoolified ways of thinking about mathematics and to circumvent the imagined rules that seemed to inhibit some parents' thinking does not indicate that we feel the mathematics curriculum is inherently inappropriate. We recognise that the curriculum is not equally accessible for all families, and to make it so would be a colossal task. Our aim therefore was to help parents think about mathematics in a different way and support those who had little confidence with curriculum (schoolified) mathematics. Our projects had the luxury of being able to explore mathematics and learning outside of the curriculum – we were not driven by what 'should' be learnt. We were able to see what activity our participants chose to describe and work with whatever experiences they brought no matter what mathematical thinking was relevant. We did not want to replicate what happens in classrooms: we deliberately wanted something different that would enable people who struggled with the curriculum to recognise and engage with mathematical concepts, ideas and ways of thinking, and see how they were a part of their everyday lives.

Stepping Away From Schoolified Mathematics

To help our participants move away from schoolified ways of thinking about mathematics, we tried to start conversations with parents by focussing on everyday activity. We hoped that this would help parents step away from their preconceptions about mathematics and be less bound in their initial thinking by their imagined rules of mathematics. This approach was not straightforward, given that we had introduced the project to schools and to participants as being about mathematics. We introduced our projects to schools as ways of supporting participants to become more comfortable with mathematical thinking, and we introduced the projects to participants in a similar way. This meant that our participants come to our workshops focussed on what they understood mathematics to be. To address this, in the Economic Activity project we had to find ways to work with children to think about mathematical activity without naming it as such – hence the introduction of the term 'economic activity'. In the Everyday Maths workshops, we instead started with a focus on family activity – this had the advantage of (1) not being specifically about mathematics and (2) being something that parents knew about but we did not, so immediately this put them in the position of experts and us in the position of learners. While this was not in and of itself sufficient to help parents step outside of schoolified ways of thinking, it was a deliberate and important part of our approach.

In both projects we were aiming to explore mathematical thinking via everyday activity. Our approach of starting with activity gave us the freedom to make interesting connections between different ideas, as they arose, and to have wide-ranging conversations. These projects were also low stakes for our participants: there was no exam and no overt negative outcomes for participants if they did not grasp new ideas or ways of thinking. This again helped us emphasise the 'not school' way of thinking about mathematics.

In the Everyday Maths project, we worked towards parents having conversations with their children about mathematics involved in everyday activity.

There are many different ways in which parents might start a conversation with their children, some of which might lead to a greater awareness of mathematic ideas and others of which might not. Even if only one conversation out of several resulted in some new awareness, then we saw that as success. Further, as the Everyday Maths project progressed, we became aware that conversations that incorporated mathematical concepts also incorporated other subjects, such as science, geography, history, language, art, music and so on. Parents initially expressed anxiety around this – it apparently contravened one of the imagined rules about mathematics. Through discussion, however, we came to the conclusion that in our project curriculum boundaries were not important. Instead, we valued the interesting conversations that supported the development of thinking, and we did not focus on classifying the learning and thinking under one specific curriculum subject. This, however, raises questions about how we encouraged people to take part in the project in the first place. We used mathematics as the focus and our participants joined the project with particular expectations about what we would be discussing. This meant that when we started focussing on activity that was not overtly mathematically focussed, parents became anxious. As discussed above, though, where mathematics is used in everyday life it is rarely discrete from other subjects and fields – so where we ended up was perhaps more representative of what 'everyday maths' really is.

It is helpful at this point to take a step back and reflect on what we were trying to do and where we got to. In both our projects we were trying to:

• Understand more about the mathematics that people use in their everyday lives.
• Understand how they can be supported to recognise this as mathematical thinking.
• Use this understanding to support children's mathematics learning outside of the school curriculum.

One of our goals was to design principles for developing support for parents, to empower them in supporting their children's learning. Goodall and Montgomery's (2014) continuum of parental involvement with schooling (where parents interact with the school around school-based activity, often on school premises) to parental engagement with learning (where parents engage with their children's learning in a much broader sense than just what is happening in school) is helpful to define what we were doing. Schools sometimes tend to encourage parental activity that is focussed around school-based involvement (Goodall & Montgomery, 2014). As the Everyday Maths project found, parents can struggle with involvement in schooling (particularly in mathematics) due to not being familiar with their children's school curriculum and not knowing how to act as a teacher for their children (Jay et al., 2018). Our work highlights the importance of parental engagement with learning, rather than involvement in schooling: learning encompasses a far wider range of activity than that which is involved in schooling (Goodall, 2022). Stepping beyond the idea of parental involvement in schooling, towards the broader idea of parental engagement in learning, can help to support families that struggle to help their children through adhering closely to school-focussed agendas. Schools do of course have a great deal of expertise in learning: we are not dismissing that or negating the importance of that. Schools are also able to encourage parents to become involved and engaged in their children's learning. As we have explained, though, doing so along curricular lines (which is what schools are familiar with and focussed on) can be a challenge for some parents.

We are proposing a different, additional way of parents engaging in their children's learning that positions parents with valuable expertise in addition to the provisions of the curriculum. For parental engagement in learning to be successful, parents need to be treated as experts. We are seeking to change rhetoric around involvement and engagement in learning that goes beyond parents solely acting in service of the school's curriculum. Our work has involved us exploring everyday family activity, considering the range of understanding that underpins that, understanding parents' emotional reactions to and intellectual interactions with that activity, and considering how to harness that to support learning.

Chapter 8

Exploring Uncertain Territory: Stepping Into the Unknown

This chapter outlines the unpredictable pathway our research followed, for us as researchers and for our participants, and how the research relationships we developed helped us to navigate that. The endeavour of researching out-of-school learning places researchers in unforseeable, uncertain and at times unknowable territory. The context of school is, to some extent, predictable and structured. This means that research activity can be planned around that context: researchers can know in advance what kinds of activities people are likely to be doing, when and where they will be doing them and what the agenda of that activity might be. Researching families' everyday lives, however, does not provide such predictability. We cannot know in advance what people do in their everyday lives, or when, where, how and why they do it. This means that it is hard to design context-appropriate research methods before a research project begins: everyday lives have so much potential for variation so it is impossible to predict in advance what kinds of methods would be most appropriate for participants to engage with, and for researchers to use. Participants in researching out-of-school learning, then, have a significant role to play in helping researchers understand this context (Clark & Laing, 2022). As we progressed through the Economic Activity project and through the Everyday Maths project, then, and gained more of a sense of how we could access an understanding of participants' family lives our projects' focus and methods took shape.

The emergent and responsive nature of our projects' design and focus meant that we could not predict or explain in advance exactly what shape our projects would take, and what we would ask of participants. This meant that our participants had to trust us: we had to persuade them that we were doing something that was worth engaging in (even though we did not know exactly what that would be), and that we would help them to develop positive outcomes from participation. Alongside the unknowns around what participation would involve, we also expected our participants to reframe the way they thought about mathematics. We didn't know exactly what this would entail, just that we wanted to move away from the boundaries of school or curriculum-focussed ways of thinking about mathematics. This represented another step into the unknown:

Parental Engagement and Out-of-School Mathematics Learning, 93–107
Copyright © 2023 Tim Jay and Jo Rose
Published under exclusive licence by Emerald Publishing Limited
doi:10.1108/978-1-78769-705-820231008

alongside the unknown of what activity would be involved in participation, we were also working with a conceptual unknown in terms of the potential impact of the project on participants. This, of course, was grounds for further uncertainty for participants and for us as researchers. The context of our projects, then, demanded that we were able to work with uncertainty, and that our participants trusted us enough to join us in that uncertainty. Berger (2015) explores the complexities of researching unfamiliar fields, and points to the importance of relationships in that.

As researchers, then, we needed to build relationships with our participants to enable trust to develop. The uncertainty and unpredictability that we experienced also points to the importance of our relationships with each other, as researchers working alongside each other. We needed to trust each other to respond flexibly and appropriately as the project developed, and be able to react positively to unexpected circumstances. Taking time to build these participant–researcher and researcher–researcher relationships helped us to become comfortable in each other's company. This made it easier to navigate our way through the uncertainty (Guillemin et al., 2018). This illustrates the tricky line that many participatory (and similar) researchers tread, between research relationship and something towards friendship – where does building rapport cross a line? But does this run the risk of silencing or inhibiting those parents who were harder to strike a rapport with? Wilson et al. (2018) discuss the potential blurring of boundaries between researcher relationship and friendship – We had to position ourselves in a place where participants could be relaxed, open up and be confident, but still maintain some sense of the temporal, research-based relationship, rather than friendship. This can be difficult to negotiate, if, for example, you want to be friends or genuinely like a participant but don't continue the relationship.

Participants' existing relationships with each other also appeared to play a role when we were asking them to explore new ideas and new ways of thinking. In the workshops in some of our schools, there were changing patterns of attendance across the different sessions. Sometimes a new participant would turn up or another not be able to make it. This changed the dynamic of a group: in those where participants knew each other already, conversations seemed to flow well and participants were happy to try out new ideas. Taking steps into the unknown, negotiating unfamiliar territory and sharing experiences were all activities where it seemed easier for participants who already knew the people they were interacting with. At times it was hard not to question our approach when sessions were less 'buzzy' or where one person dominated the conversation. We had to respond to the context of each session, taking into account the individuals in the room and their relationships with each other. We held conversations that may not have been explicitly furthering our research agenda but were important in developing and maintaining relationships with and between our participants. We believed that the sense of risk, of vulnerability, of exposure, of trepidation, that comes from not quite knowing what you are doing and what the result will be, would likely to be less if our participants felt comfortable around us, as well as around each other. Our experience of this in workshops was echoed in our later work with teachers, where we have tried to share the ideas that lay behind the projects and think about how the ideas could be taken forward into schools. Where teachers knew each other, it seemed easier for them to share ideas and be more spontaneous when reframing their thinking.

Our projects asked participants to step outside of what they knew and how they thought about maths. As researchers, we were also stepping outside of what we knew – in terms of being able to predict what form our data would take and how best to elicit those data, and in terms of knowing what change we expected to result from the project. Our uncertainty involved a shift in our understanding of what it means to be researchers, and working alongside each other helped us develop confidence that it was ok to be going through this process.

Boundary Concepts and Intellectual Shifts

This process of working together to take steps into the unknown can be better understood by using boundary concepts as a tool. In particular, boundary crossing (Akkerman & Bakker, 2011) and boundary experiences (Clark et al., 2017) are useful in considering how individuals with different perspectives position themselves, in terms of activity, in terms of role and particularly in terms of intellectual shifts.

The idea of boundary crossing relates to learning that happens when people with different ideas come together and share their perspectives. Akkerman and Bakker's (2011) review draws on literature that mainly focussed on professional activity and identified processes involved when learning happens at the boundaries of professionals' existing understanding. The key point is that individuals who come together for a shared endeavour have similarities in terms of what they are trying to achieve. There are also differences, however, that create boundaries between those individuals in terms of what they know and do, and how they think and act. Boundary crossing as a concept is well used in research on collaborative learning. In particular, cultural–historical activity theory (Engeström, 1987) uses boundary crossing to discuss what happens when two different activity systems (or ways of thinking about and enacting practice) come together. Wenger's (1998) concept of communities of practice also explores how people from different backgrounds working on a shared endeavour come to shift their framing of problems and practice to new shared ways of thinking.

Both cultural–historical activity theory and communities of practice tend to incorporate discussion of boundary crossing as part of the wider context. Akkerman and Bakker (2011), however, zoom in to focus on the steps of change involved when boundary crossing happens. They identify four main stages: identification; coordination; reflection and transformation.

Identification involves recognising points of difference around role, practice, knowledge and understanding, and concepts used to think about a problem. These points of difference may lie between individuals or within an individual across different contexts. Recognition of this difference is important in delineating professional territory, enabling people to feel secure in their role and contribution. This also relates to Rose (2011), who outlined that successful inter-professional work may entail some element of stepping back from role, expertise, territory and power. *Coordination* involves using the communication structures and practices between individuals so differences can be acknowledged, and translation so that individuals can understand each others' roles, practices, knowledge and concepts. Through coordination, individuals can more easily navigate the boundaries that delineate difference and develop ways of working effectively together. *Reflection* plays another core role in boundary crossing. Akkerman and Bakker (2011) highlight how this involves perspective making and perspective taking – individuals being explicit about their role and practices, to enable others to see things from their perspective. When working on a shared problem, the ability to view it from different angles through this kind of dialogic practice can lead to new and creative ways to address challenges. Ultimately, successful boundary crossing can be framed as *transformation*. Working with others to address shared challenges can be disruptive and confront existing ways of thinking. Coming together through a process of identification, coordination and reflection can lead to new ways of thinking and working, and making those explicit in our practices. Continuous joint work at boundaries is likely to lead to transformation of thinking and practice.

These boundary crossing concepts are helpful to highlight how we came together with different perspectives in our projects and engaged with those differences to develop our thinking about the nature of mathematics, and about research more generally. In our projects, there were differences in what we (researchers and participants) recognised as mathematics and our beliefs about how it related to the school curriculum. There were also differences in how we (as researchers) believed research should be constructed. Through the dialogic processes that happened in the workshops and in our research team discussions, we attempted to make those differences explicit and to recognise the value in different perspectives. This led to us thinking about mathematics and about research in different ways. Engaging with different ways of framing what mathematics is and what research is, that lay outside the boundaries of our existing thinking was an important part of our research. We were trying to support our participants to step outside of the boundary of 'what they knew' about what mathematics is – and also through this work, we reframed our own understanding. Boundary crossing, then, became fundamental to what we were trying to do. Each actor in our research (each researcher, each participant) held a different set of understanding and ways of thinking about mathematics (and for us, about research as well), and it is at the boundary between these ways of thinking that we became most productive.

The use of boundary concepts to understand our learning is interesting because we were not working with two explicit 'knowns' that fall either side of a boundary. During our conversations with participants, we became interested in their beliefs about what mathematics is, and this is not especially easy to articulate. When working with participants we reflected on our beliefs about what mathematics is, and our participants' beliefs, and tried to permeate the boundaries between those ways of thinking. We hoped to come to new ways of understanding how to think about, recognise and discuss everyday maths. This was similar to the dynamics of how participants interacted with each other in their discussions: they also worked to permeate boundaries of how they thought about everyday maths. We worked with participants to identify differences in ways of thinking, coordinate the communication and understanding of those differences, reflect on how others view everyday maths and thus transform our ways of thinking. Boundary crossing concepts, then, can illustrate the ways in which we sought to develop our thinking about mathematics. This is a disruptive process by necessity. We needed to move on in our thinking so that we could more fully understand the nature of everyday maths and how it can be used to help develop learning conversations in the family. The element of disruption is important: we knew that existing ways of thinking weren't helpful, so we deliberately tried to step outside our boundaries to develop a new perspective.

Clark et al. (2017) expanded Akkerman and Bakker's (2011) discussion of boundary concepts, introducing the ideas of boundary experiences. These are the shared experiences between people who work in different ways: in Clark et al.'s (2017) work, this involved researchers conducting interdisciplinary and co-production research, where researchers with different experiences and world views came together on the same project. Clark et al. discuss how the reciprocal conversations that happen in the experience of coming together are helpful in stimulating transformation. The idea of reciprocity is important: for people to be motivated in these boundary experiences, it helps if everyone can learn, benefit from and develop through the encounter, rather than the exchange being just one way. Boundary experiences are more important than the boundary objects (the shared problem that is the focus of the work) in mutual transformation, to help reframe thinking and change practice (Clark et al., 2017). This emphasis on the importance of reciprocal, dialogic relationships in transformation again aligns with our work: we were dependent on our experiences with each other (participant/researcher, participant/participant, researcher/researcher) to highlight differences in our thinking and concepts. The discussions we had about the boundaries between others' ways of thinking and our own existing conceptual frameworks helped to push and reshape our thinking. In our work, these differences highlighted by the boundaries were crucial. We needed to acknowledge different ways of thinking about mathematics and about research, we needed to be comfortable with and curious about that difference and work with it to develop new ways of framing everyday maths and expand our ideas around what researching that entailed.

In this process, we had to explore and explain our existing ideas about what everyday maths is, what our priorities in our research were and listen to others to help stimulate and develop our own thinking. We were all trying to take our thinking forward in some way. We were trying to reconceptualise how we thought about out-of-school maths, and as researchers we were working at the boundary of what we knew about 'how to be' researchers in that context. We were therefore trying to change that boundary, or even step beyond it to expand our understanding of what everyday maths is and what it means to be a researcher of everyday maths. This is less about the boundaries between us as individual researchers, and more about boundaries between what we knew and how we were as researchers, and what we didn't know. Put another way, it was about the boundaries of what we currently understood as research, and the unknown. This means that Akkerman and Bakker's (2011) work on boundary crossing concepts is perhaps less helpful than Clark et al.'s (2017) concept of boundary experiences when considering how we developed as researchers. The four boundary crossing aspects highlighted by Akkerman and Bakker (2011), of identification, coordination, reflection and transformation, are easier to consider in terms of two people working on either side of a boundary. For us, as researchers, the boundary was between our own understanding, and what we didn't know: in a sense, we were both positioned on the same side of the boundary. The opportunity to push those boundaries came from articulating our thinking to and with each other, and reflecting on our changing understanding about the nature of out-of-school learning and out-of-school maths. The emphasis here was on experience and interaction: hence why Clark et al.'s (2017) concept of boundary experiences is helpful for thinking about our transformation as researchers. The shared experiences and conversations we had are what led to the transformation of our concepts: this arose in part at least from our understanding and thinking about what we were trying to do, and from our aim to traverse the boundary of what we knew into the territory of what we didn't know.

This consideration of boundaries emphasises the importance of relationships in our work. We needed to be comfortable that there were boundaries and differences between us as individuals, and between us and the unknown, and comfortable with the idea of trying to cross those boundaries. We had a well-established professional relationship with each other (and with Ben, who was the researcher on the Everyday Maths project) that was not solely agenda-driven. This gave us a secure base from which to consider difference, to work with the uncertainty of crossing boundaries, and to have experiences in those unknown spaces. We were comfortable to have meandering conversations that may or may not take us anywhere useful – we could explore ideas and boundaries and territory in an unstructured and spontaneous way, and our professional familiarity with each other meant that we had a safe basis from which to do this.

This familiarity and ease in each others' company took time to develop. Before the project started, we had reading groups, where we discussed specific relevant papers, what we liked and didn't like about them and how they made us think. We spent time socialising – going out for lunch and coffee together, talking about things that weren't necessarily directly related to the project. We each kept a reflective journal where we noted down our own experiences of Everyday Maths, responses to activities we had done as part of the project, ideas that occurred to us, questions we had and challenges we were experiencing. We shared what we wrote in those journals with each other. We also explicitly discussed our openness to seeing how the project progressed: while we all had a broad sense that we wanted to support parents to use their existing expertise to support their children's mathematical understanding, we weren't sure on what route we would take to achieve this. This process of relationship development was more involved than it was with our participants, but we still put time into getting to know the parents we worked with. We spent time getting to know them in the playground before we started running the workshops. We started each workshop with tea and coffee and chat, before gradually moving on to the 'research business' of discussing everyday maths.

Spending time on making relationships more secure – with each other, and with our participants – also helped us feel safer in negotiating uncertain territory. Learning to think in new ways and trying to reframe our understanding felt, for us, to some extent destabilising and risky, and working alongside each other – who we knew and trusted – helped to mitigate this. This builds on Blix and Wettergren's (2015) work on the emotional labour that underpins qualitative research, specifically foregrounding the relational work that is needed. For us, paying attention to the relational work then meant that the process of exploring uncertain territory together, in turn, served to develop those relationships further. There was a reciprocal link between our researcher relationships and navigating uncertainty.

In developing relationships with our participants and with each other, we progressed as researchers and traversed several boundaries. These boundaries delineated the ways we thought about what mathematics was, its place in everyday life and how we reconstructed our roles as researchers. We moved between leading or facilitating the sessions, to thinking *with* our participants. We started the project with different ways of constructing what we were doing, but over the duration of the project (and after) we continued to reflect together, and shifted our ways of thinking. These boundary experiences, then, were dependent on relationships in our quest for transformation – and the process of trans-formation also helped to strengthen those relationships. The nature of our rela-tionships enabled us to have boundary experiences that moved our thinking forward into the unknown. Of course, learning and developing thinking is always about exploring the unknown for any individual who is doing the learning. For us, however, none of us knew exactly where we were going with our thinking. We were exploring and transforming and bringing our thinking together, from different starting points. We were working at the boundaries of what we knew and trying to step beyond those boundaries to make sense of the unknown.

Developing and Maintaining the Relationships Needed for Transformational Boundary Experiences

Relationships, then, were hugely important in our research. Even though the longitudinal element was only short term in both our projects, we still needed to reflect on and respond to how the relational dynamics played out over time and consider the impact of this on the research process. Longitudinal projects often encourage (and require) researcher reflexivity (Thomson & Holland, 2003), and the highly relational nature of our work brought this into sharp relief. Our reflexivity as researchers played a significant role in determining the direction of our projects. We needed to reflect on relational dynamics as the project pro-gressed, we needed to understand our participants and their reactions and use the capital of our relationships to understand how best to steer and develop the project as we went along.

Building relationships with participants helped them feel more comfortable sharing their thinking with us and likely enhanced their trust in us to take the project in appropriate directions (even though we weren't quite sure ourselves where we were taking it). Reciprocity, though, was important in these relationships: we were trying to help participants to develop their own understanding about maths, and at the same time we were dependent on them (and on each other) to help us to develop our understanding about how maths is thought about, and our understanding about what direction the research should or could take. This sense of reciprocity was important to bolster the relationship and help position us as 'partners' in the process of understanding everyday maths. In our work, researchers and participants each brought their own expertise, rather than us being positioned as 'teachers' and participants as 'learners' (which was a dynamic we actively tried to avoid). Participants brought expertise in their everyday activity, and in their thinking about everyday maths. We brought the methods for developing that thinking. We were all using participants' knowledge (they were sharing it with each other, and with us) and we were all using discursive and reflective methods (participants to develop their thinking about maths, us to develop our thinking about how people think about maths, and our thinking about research and research methods). In this way, we all contributed to the project and we all learnt from it. We still held power in terms of the direction of the research. Nonetheless, our responsiveness to participants and to the context, in terms of how and where we steered our projects, and our determination not to impose a pre-determined research structure onto our participants, probably contributed to the continued engagement of our participants (Thomson & Holland, 2003).

The way in which research relationships impact on the shaping of both physical and semantic spaces was highlighted by Clark et al. (2017). Semantic space relates to language used: developing researcher and participant thinking together supports the creation of a shared language and shared semantic space. We suggest that this is just a part of a broader concept of intellectual space, which is not just focussed on language but also on the ideas and ways of thinking that we hold and develop. These intellectual spaces can also develop and change through our interactions with others: similar to how Edwards (2011) describes relational agency, when interaction with others can change the way we think and conceptualise problems, and how we work to solve them.

In our project, we had to understand what Clark et al. (2017) describe as existing codes of behaviour and consider how or whether we integrated those into our thinking. For us, the school code or school-focussed way of doing things was an important consideration. We wanted to step outside of the school code of mathematics learning and outside the school code of the teacher/learner dynamic. This felt unusual, and a little unsafe and destabilising, largely because it was unknown and unpredictable, and we had no set plan of what should happen. The unknown is a slightly scary place to be, but stepping outside of those known codes meant that we were able to combine and transform agendas (our agendas and those of our participants), and it gave us flexibility. For this to work, however, we (participants and researchers) had to be brave about the uncertainty, and sound relationships gave us stability on which to build that bravery and make use of the flexibility.

In highlighting the importance of relationships in our projects, it is important to remember that the characteristics of those involved had a strong influence on the research practices and direction of the projects. Our individual attributes and ways of thinking, and those of our participants, influenced how our shared cognitions developed. This influenced the research practices that we developed and the direction we took the projects. Our projects shaped the way they did because of who we were and who our participants were. It would be naïve to try to precisely duplicate the projects and the pathways that they followed: we would be different people to who we were at the start of our projects, and we would be working with different participants with different characteristics. This means that encouraging others to use our ideas is challenging, of course: the project is not exactly replicable because it depends on the characteristics and interactions of those involved. This also means that the outcomes from another version of the project would be uncertain. However, what we can do is share the broad principles that we worked with and encourage people to take those forward in their own way – this will be discussed further in Chapter 10.

The Link Between Agenda and Relationships

The nature of the relationships in our projects played a key role in shaping the direction of our research. The previous section uses Clark et al.'s (2017) concept of boundary experiences to help consider why and how relationships are important in transforming participants' thinking and our own thinking. It is also useful, however, to reflect on the nature of our research and how this relates to the role that relationships played. Our research was to a large extent exploratory. We were not seeking to confirm pre-existing ideas: we had the flexibility of a more open agenda and our research design allowed for that. With this flexibility came the reliance on relationships, and the space to focus on those relationships. It is also important, however, to consider our participants' agendas for being involved in the project. While our agenda was flexible, we knew that we didn't want to focus on school maths, yet some of our participants were expecting us to do so. We needed to face the complexities of not knowing exactly where our project was going, but also consider that we wanted to avoid focussing on school mathematics even though some of our participants were expecting or wanting us to do so. The uncertainty meant that we couldn't tell them exactly what we would end up focussing on, but we hoped it would be interesting and useful even though it wasn't school mathematics. This complexity around agendas again highlights the crucial role of trusting relationships in our projects.

These relationships helped us to feel more secure when taking steps into the unknown. They helped us (as researchers) to feel more confident in steering the project as we went along, and participants to feel more confident in joining us on that journey. We wanted to steer the project ourselves, and control the direction, but we also wanted our participants to buy into that, to take them along with us and for them to provoke and stimulate our thinking. It is important for research participants to feel as though their participation will make a difference to things they care about (Flewitt et al., 2018), even though (as in our case) they may not be overtly steering the project. For us, we hoped that participation would enable families to engage more confidently with mathematical concepts and learning more generally in the family, and would maybe (ultimately – although well beyond the scope of the project) feed into children's attainment in school. We wanted participants to feel that this was a likely outcome, but what we were doing was not overtly focussed on what families recognised as school mathematics.

We wanted to support participants to step away from school mathematics, to develop their understanding of Everyday Maths and support them to become more confident in doing so. As researchers, we needed to step away from school mathematics and not focus on it too: we wanted to work together with our participants to explore other ways of thinking and learning. Investment in relationships, then, was an important part of our work, especially in the Everyday Maths project. This will be familiar to many researchers who engage in participant-led research (e.g. Israel et al., 2017; Rose & Todd, 2022). Although our research was steered by us, rather than being participant-led, we still needed to develop informal research relationships. These helped us to understand the research context and to reflect on how to respond to the ongoing complexities and uncertainties within the projects. We needed to be able to respond to the ideas and concepts that arose as we interacted with participants – and we could not predict in advance what these would be.

As researchers, we shifted our expectations and agenda about what would be feasible to achieve with our participants and how that needed to be achieved. In the Everyday Maths project, we gradually reframed our focus in some of the workshops onto learning conversations (not specifically maths) as we realised with participants that curriculum boundaries were very blurred, and singling out one subject led to anxieties about whether discussions were or were not mathematical enough. We still were aiming to support parents to be more confident in discussing ideas with their children, but as the project progressed the complexities of that became apparent. In particular, we had to break down the perceived prerequisites of confidence (around knowing the school mathematics curriculum). We needed to take time to develop our understanding of the project as it went along and use discussions with our participants and each other to consider the changing shape and direction of the project from many different angles.

The shift in agenda that we negotiated is related to the structure and purpose of our projects. They were not pre-determined, rigid designs, where the intention was to collect data in a specific, planned way and analyse them using a pre-determined method. We did collect and analyse data, of course, but the nature of those data evolved over time. This was another way in which we, as researchers, needed to become comfortable with uncertainty – and this was difficult!

Power and Participation

Our projects were responsive to our interactions with participants, but it is important to remember that they were still shaped by us as researchers pursuing our agenda: we maintained a powerful position in the research, though still recognising the need to learn from our participants. Our projects were not participatory, in terms of who set the agenda and direction of the projects. They were still dependent on successful relationships, but with different power dynamics involved than may be the case in more participatory projects.

We wanted participants to buy into our emergent agenda and wanted to shape this in response to our ongoing work with them. The extent to which participants are confident and able to share their own ideas about agenda and have them heard varies widely and (in part at least) depends on relationships. This is not only about the relationship between the researcher and participant but (as Gristy, 2015 highlights) also about the relationships between participants and their context, and the relationships between the participants themselves. All of these relationships are potentially impacted by power dynamics. The need to pay attention to power dynamics between researchers and participants, especially in qualitative research, is well documented (e.g. McGarry, 2016). The context of the research – in our case, schools – can also affect participants' engagement and sense of agency (Bayeck, 2022). Existing relationships between participants (in our case, parents) who may already know each other outside of the research project – whether as family, socially, professionally or through their involvement in the school – also contribute to the way interactions happen in research (Haines Lyon, 2022). These relationships needed careful attention as we supported participants to have their voices heard.

Our power as researchers was reflected in our control of the project: when and where it took place, what the focus was, how we steered the agenda. In the Everyday Maths project especially, it was still important that our participants had a sense of agency and expertise, so we needed to handle our power carefully. Our projects took place in schools, so we needed to pay attention to the implicit messages about roles and avoid the 'teacher/learner' dynamic, as discussed in earlier chapters. Our participants held expertise in things that we did not know about – specifically, in their everyday family lives – and we wanted them to share this with us. This highlights the difference between power and expertise: our power enabled us to steer the direction of the project, but the success of that was reliant on our participants' expertise. Yet the fact that we were powerful potentially meant that participants were less confident to share their expertise. We needed, then, to draw attention away from our powerful position and attempt to make our participants more confident.

To try to lessen this power differential, we focussed on elements of common ground and shared understandings with our participants. As researchers, we all had our own similarities to (and differences from) our participants. Working with those similarities and differences was important in terms of how we built our relationships and tried to reduce the power differential (Dhillon & Thomas, 2019). Of course, for our project to progress we needed parents to be comfortable in discussing their family experiences and be happy to take the lead in this respect. This sat somewhat uncomfortably alongside our role in directing the agenda of the project.

As researchers who knew the project, inhabiting the different roles of leading the direction of the project on the one hand and being led in our understanding of family life on the other hand was something we were able to do. Our jobs as academics prepared us for this role switching. We are practiced at working with different people in many different ways, leading in some roles and being led in others. For our participants, however, this may be more challenging. Firstly, in the school context, parents are rarely positioned as experts or taking the lead: teachers are usually the experts in the school context. The physical space we used for the Everyday Maths project was one where parents were not used to being experts. Secondly, we were asking them to step in and out of a 'leading' role, depending on which aspect of the project we were thinking about. We were saying to them at some points we wanted them to be the experts (in family activity), and at other points they had to trust us to be the experts (in designing and facilitating the activities, in explaining how the project would help them). We have sometimes considered whether our methods were predicated on our own (privileged) assumptions that people want to talk and to share their experiences. In our role as academics, we are required to make original contributions to knowledge and to share our thinking with others. We are likely, therefore, to feel that our voice is worth listening to – but this is not going to be the same for all.

We didn't explicitly discuss the strangeness of the space and the roles with parents in the Everyday Maths project. As researchers we were able to switch roles, but it was only after the project that we reflected on what this might mean for parents. At the time we were mainly focussed on trying to make those different spaces comfortable places to be for our participants. It is hard to know whether explicitly acknowledging those shifting dynamics would have been helpful or whether it could have made parents feel more awkward in the research space. Drawing explicit attention to our role as researchers may have separated us out from our participants and made it too easy to slip into the teacher/learner dynamic that we were trying to avoid. We wanted to highlight the similarities between ourselves and our participants, to help make them feel comfortable in our presence (e.g. Adu-Ampong & Adams, 2020).

The principles of insiderness (where we explicitly or implicitly highlighted similarities between ourselves and our participants) and outsiderness (where we were aware of and in some cases drew attention to the differences between ourselves and our participants) helped us position ourselves with our participants and at some points consider our 'inbetween-ness' (Milligan, 2016). We worked with insiderness in terms of how we dressed (informally), by sharing our own family activity (especially given Tim's and Ben's roles as parents), by Ben discussing his emerging understanding of how mathematics was present in his everyday life. We tried to create similarity with our participants: as one parent noted, we dressed in our 'cosy jumpers' which played down differences with participants and emphasised that we weren't in the teacher role. For the researcher, acknowledging insiderness and outsiderness is about developing sound and rich research relationships with others who are both similar and different. As with many researcher relationships, though, this is a difficult balance to strike. The very nature or role of being a researcher puts you in a different and powerful position which will obviously impact on relationships – we cannot expect research relationships to develop along the same lines as friendships that are developed in other contexts (Dhillon & Thomas, 2019). We claim nonetheless that the ability to develop relationships as a researcher is important and draws on similar social skills to those used in developing friendships or other types of relationship. The process of research, though, involves carefully treading the path of negotiating and developing relationships and position. The groups we belong to and are accepted into are not static, and this is hugely important when moving within research contexts. Group belonging is active and dynamic (Oikonomidoy & Wiest, 2017) and individuals (researchers or otherwise) enact belonging in their own ways.

In our projects, we wanted to achieve an authentic informality, in part to reduce difference and demonstrate to participants that we were in many ways like them. In that way we enacted our researcher role *as* building relationships – the skills we drew on as researchers were to a great extent relational, with of course some underpinning understanding of the concepts of informal mathematics learning. The ongoing research decisions we made were sensitive to the individuals (both researchers and participants) involved. Our relational research practice with its consideration of insider/outsider positioning highlights the relevance of competence in crossing boundaries (Clark et al., 2017) and the importance of recognising and understanding context and interactions (Oikonomidoy & Wiest, 2017).

When we came to disseminate our work and share the principles of the Everyday Maths project for others to use, the importance of positioning and relationships became very evident. When discussing who might be best placed to roll out our ideas, we of course considered schools. However, schools have a clearly established power dynamic in relationships with families – the school agenda is usually what is important, and schools are not used to giving away the direction of that agenda. Furthermore, parents (and children) are not used to having the opportunity to shape their own agenda. Schools form part of statutory provision – as highlighted by Clark et al. (2017) – so they have a particular code or way of working. Such codes in statutory provision tend to be established and difficult to change or break out of. Schools also have established relationships with parents that work (necessarily) with different dynamics to those of our project. This all means that schools cannot mirror what we did and cannot build relationships with participants in the same way. It can still be helpful, however, to make explicit the relational issues that underpin projects such as Everyday Maths. Reflecting on the shared and separate physical, semantic and relational spaces that are inhabited, and considering how the boundaries between those spaces can be blurred, may help schools and parents to step into a different relational space. Critical friends can help in reflecting on and negotiating these boundaries (Hedges, 2010), so both researchers and teachers can consider what their practices are, how those practices are received by others and from there effect change.

Being Comfortable With the Unknown

The uncertain territory that we found ourselves in, and the relationships that helped us negotiate that uncertainty, fed into our development as researchers. We both have backgrounds in psychology. This is a discipline that teaches structured research methods, with designs that are for the most part controlled and predictable and have measurable outcomes (e.g. Coolican, 2018). We were both comfortable stepping outside traditional scientific methods, but these projects took us a step beyond our previous experience. We were not working with objectively measurable outcomes, and some stakeholders (funders and schools) seemed disappointed that we did not focus on children's attainment. Further, our projects (especially Everyday Maths) used methods that could not be pre-defined. In both projects we started with conventional surveys and focus groups to help us understand participants' ways of thinking and give us an insight into their activities. The main parts of both projects, however, used methods that developed and clarified as the project progressed. It is probably no coincidence that these methods led to deeper conceptual shifts in our thinking.

Writing concisely about these methods (and the resultant shifts in our understanding) is not easy, however. There is no shorthand that describes what we did, in a way that could be easily reproduced by others – in part because the methods were emergent and developed in response to the dynamics of the relationships. When describing and writing about the projects, it is very difficult to name the methods that we used and how we made our decisions: the nature of the projects emerged through discussions between the project team (and at times with the participants in the sessions) as the research progressed. This approach does not fit neatly into a disciplinary tradition. Some social science researchers will recognise and be familiar with these principles of working, but others may challenge the rigour of such approaches (Keiner, 2019).

In order to work like this, we had to feel secure with our own abilities as researchers. We had to trust that we had the skills to be able to be responsive and to allow things to develop as we went along and the resources to make appropriate decisions. We needed to accept the uncertainty in our project trajectories: in a sense, we had to be comfortable with the idea of being uncomfortable. Although from psychology, we were comfortable with interdisciplinarity, we have backgrounds of using mixed methods in educational research and of conducting different types of research that entails (or at least benefits from) developing strong relationships with participants. These characteristics and past experiences helped us negotiate the uncertainty in methods. Here we return again to how our identity as researchers, and the combination of our expertise and experiences, shaped the projects' methods and trajectories.

It is likely that our soft skills of collaboration and relationship building were just as important as our methodological expertise and experience, especially in the Everyday Maths project. These skills were important in allowing us to step back and be led by parents. In this project, we framed parents' expertise as (1) in their activity and (2) in wanting to develop a different relationship with maths. Our expertise centred on group facilitation, understanding maths in context and reassuring parents that uncertainty and unpredictability is ok. It was important to communicate that it was ok to not 'know the answer' in terms of maths, and that it was ok to not know exactly where the project was leading. Relationships, then, were not only important between us as researchers and the participants but also between ourselves as a research team (Bossio et al., 2014). We had to trust each other that we could find our way through the uncertainty and the project would work out ok in the end. The time spent building relationships is crucial to any project, but especially to ones with elements of uncertainty.

Our experience highlights that developing relationships with others is a generic research skill that it is important to learn and practice. This is well documented in terms of the importance of developing rapport with participants (Collins & Cooper, 2014), but the generic research skill of getting along with co-researchers, institutional colleagues who support the research process, funders and other stakeholders beyond participants can go unnoticed and is not often considered in depth. This may be because, as a concept, it is hard to define – what does 'being good at developing relationships' mean, what does it entail? As researchers, we need to be able to move easily through our research contexts. In qualitative work particularly, we need to get to know our participants, we need to encourage authenticity, we need to be open to others' ways of thinking and we need to be aware of how others (participants, stakeholders, collaborators) respond to us. We need to be able to get along with others to produce good quality data. But is this something that can be taught? Perhaps people who find developing relationships easy are more likely than others to be drawn to qualitative research. Our projects needed us to develop relationships to help negotiate the uncertainty, but that same uncertainty also gave us flexibility to spend time and energy developing those relationships, and this is something we enjoyed.

Chapter 9

The Ethics of Disruption

This chapter will explore the many ways in which our projects acted as a catalyst for disruption. The process of negotiating uncertain territory (see Chapter 8) impacted on participants, on funders, on how we packaged the research to share it with others and ultimately on our own thinking as researchers. In this chapter, we consider whether our projects should be described as research or as intervention, or as both. We reflect on the potential of such projects to disrupt our thinking and through that disruption help us to reframe our understanding of the field.

As highlighted in earlier chapters, our projects were not directly focussed on pupil attainment or curriculum mathematics. In the process of developing the projects, we had to work hard to shift children's and parents' expectations about the nature of mathematics: these expectations were based on experiences of school mathematics. Our projects focussed on mathematical thinking that was inherent in everyday activity: we have explained in previous chapters how this differs from the school curriculum. Nonetheless, schools were still interested in being involved in our projects because of the potential for the activities to support children's learning in the classroom. Schools acted as gatekeepers, supporting our access to participants. This meant that participants were likely to frame their expectations about the projects with reference to school. We needed, therefore, to make concerted efforts to position the projects to participants as 'not-school mathematics', as we have discussed in previous chapters.

In the Everyday Maths project, this was also the focus of some of our discussions with our funders. We needed to clarify that the Everyday Maths project was different from projects that aimed to involve parents in the school curriculum. The focus of our work also meant that it was unrealistic to expect pupils' attainment to improve as a result of the projects – at least in the short or medium term. Our methods meant that we could explore qualitative differences in participants' thinking and reported motivation. We could propose that this may lead to improved pupil engagement and attainment in curricular maths in the long term given that there are associations between student engagement and achievement (Heffner & Antaramian, 2016; Pekrun et al., 2002), but we did not have the scope in our projects to explore whether this actually happens. The methods that we used, however, meant that we could be responsive to needs of our participants in different schools, with resultant benefits for participant engagement. Our

Parental Engagement and Out-of-School Mathematics Learning, 109–122
Copyright © 2023 Tim Jay and Jo Rose
Published under exclusive licence by Emerald Publishing Limited
doi:10.1108/978-1-78769-705-820231009

methods meant that our participants engaged in our projects and enabled us to make claims about the ways people engage with everyday maths and how confidence in doing so could be developed. These same methods, however, did not allow us to make resultant claims about improvement in curricular attainment.

The emergent and unpredictable nature of the projects, as described in Chapter 8, meant that the projects developed in different ways across different schools. In the Economic Activity project, this was reflected in the nature of the data (see Chapter 3), where different schools with different demographics yielded data with very different characteristics. In the Everyday Maths project, parents' motivations for engaging in the project – which again seemed related to demographics – led to us working in different schools in different ways, as described in Chapter 4. To develop a sense of mutual engagement with parents, we had to respond to different circumstances and develop a range of ways of working. Even if we had held a clear plan for the Everyday Maths workshops from the start, we could not have stuck to that plan in every school, as different parents engaged with the project's ideas in different ways.

This uncertainty was challenging for us, as researchers, and perhaps for some participants too. Such uncertainty can also be difficult for those who fund research. The funders of the Economic Activity project set out to fund projects which had an element of risk: this project was presented from the outset as something that was potentially exciting but untested, and therefore the outcomes were uncertain. When writing the funding application for the Everyday Maths project, we had presented the workshops as action research, taking place in collaboration with parents and teachers. We said that the workshops would be informed by the outcomes of the survey and focus groups, but ultimately 'led by participants'. We had indicated in the funding proposal that as well as increased enthusiasm from parents, we hoped to see an increase in children's interest, motivation and achievement in mathematics and wanted to produce guides for children as well as parents on involvement in out-of-school mathematics. However, as the project progressed, we realised that this was unrealistic and the project was not as straightforward as it appeared in our application. We needed to work with the funders, then, to justify the uncertain trajectory of the project as it progressed.

In the process of dissemination, we began to recognise that our methods were (at least slightly) radical. It was difficult to write concisely about the methods and findings of such complex projects in single papers and to locate the work in specific bodies of knowledge. What we were trying to do and what we were finding out was not straightforward: we have attempted to communicate some of this complexity in this book. There was no shorthand for the methods we used – we were working responsively and relationally, so did not follow a set procedure. Similarly, our findings are best viewed at the macro level, in order to pull together our understanding from across the projects to reframe the way we think about out-of-school mathematical activity.

The funders for the Everyday Maths project wanted us to package our recommendations on how to run workshops in schools, and we had included the development of a 'toolkit' for schools as part of our application. When considering the dynamics of the workshops, however, we questioned how best to make a toolkit for workshops that used emergent and relational methods and required confident facilitators who would avoid a teacher/pupil dynamic. As discussed in earlier chapters, the workshops developed as they did because of who we were as individuals and because of the nature of the interactions between us and our participants. If others were to facilitate, the workshops would inevitably pan out in different ways. We felt that the responsiveness to context and the relationality were important characteristics of the workshops – so packaging the process into a toolkit for schools inevitably simplified the complexity and glossed over the nuance of our interactions. It is doubtful, then, that the workshops could be easily replicated by others, although the principles we used could be followed to different ends.

In sharing our workshop methods, we considered who would be in a good position to facilitate them. We felt it was important that facilitators were confident in mathematics, which – when it comes to primary school staff – points to teachers. However, as discussed in earlier chapters, we had to work hard to step outside of the teacher/learner dynamic in the workshops. It was important that parents led with their expertise on family activity, yet if teachers were facilitating the workshops, then it would be harder for parents to see the workshop facilitators as anything but teachers.

The discussions around mathematical thinking in the Everyday Maths workshops needed to be led by parents and therefore start from the nature of family activity, rather than from specific mathematical concepts. In our early attempts to disseminate our work on the project, we tried running sessions with teachers to explain the process we used in the workshops. We emphasised the way in which we started with everyday activity and took an opportunistic approach to discussing the mathematical thinking that arose in this activity. In these sessions, however, teachers' automatic response was to start with curriculum concepts. Rather than starting with discussions about what they and their families or friends did, they sought for and framed specific activity in terms of which mathematical concepts it could illustrate. This reflects teachers' everyday role – in their day-to-day work they are focussed on the curriculum, and asking them to change the nature of what they do is a significant undertaking. We also need to consider whether the kind of open-ended exploration and thinking, with no real agenda in mind, is something that is easy for teachers and parents (and researchers!) to do. It can be difficult to justify time spent discussing what we did at the weekend, without a clearly defined outcome. Time spent just exploring ideas with no clear end point in mind feels like a luxury and is something that we are not familiar with doing.

This focus on open-ended exploration with no fixed agenda, and no certain outcome, meant that it was hard to assess the impact of what we were doing. We were hoping to influence the ways families recognised maths in their everyday activity and the kinds of conversations they had. But this kind of outcome is hard to identify, hard to observe and almost impossible to measure. Additionally, the workshops took different shapes with different groups of parents and different facilitators in different schools – so it would be unrealistic to expect workshops to impact on participants in the same ways, even if it were feasible to observe impact.

The unpredictability of the workshops, then, alongside the unpredictable range of outcomes of the project, raises questions about how to persuade potential funders that this kind of project is worth funding. This is especially taxing because the projects did not necessarily conform to a standard research or intervention format. In considering the outcomes of the projects, we also recognised that they do not sit comfortably with the current (linear) impact agenda and assumptions of universities (McCowan, 2018): the outcomes were not easily standardised or measurable, and there was no standard intervention that is easily transferable from one context to another. Chapter 8 describes how as researchers, we had to become comfortable with uncertainty: we were not sure how the projects would develop and how participants would respond. We did not know what impact the projects would have on participants, but we had to be enthusiastic to get people on board. We hoped it would be a good use of everybody's time, but we were not sure. We hoped that our work would effect positive change for families, but we were not sure that it would. We hoped that we would be able to work with different groups of participants and their agendas, but we did not know what those would be. Our discussions within the research team, where we explored these issues as the project progressed, helped us to manage all these uncertainties and shape the projects as we went along.

The extent to which we were explicit with participants, schools and funders about the extremely exploratory nature of our projects – in particular the Everyday Maths project – varied. This was in part because the uncertainty became more evident as we moved through the project. Essentially, we are trying to understand as we went along how we should work with parents to effect positive change. We were more explicit about that with parents than schools. Some of this relates to us not actually understanding what we were doing until we were doing it – and parents were obviously directly involved in the workshops where we (as researchers) were doing that learning. There was no representation, however, from schools at the workshops. This meant that schools were not involved in the process of shaping the trajectory of the projects and they were probably less aware of the uncertainty, and of how we were negotiating that uncertainty.

The ways we worked with parents in the Everyday Maths project were different to the way that schools tend to position their engagement with parents. In another project working with parents and schools, Haines Lyon (2022) found that schools took parental engagement seriously but positioned this as relatively passive, with parents listening to and following the school agenda. More active engagement by parents in education can be seen as destabilising, with parents shaping their own ideas and potentially questioning the school's agenda. In the Everyday Maths project, however, we worked towards active engagement (in Haines Lyon's terms) to support parents to develop their own ways of thinking and move away from curriculum mathematics.

While schools in the Everyday Maths project were happy to act as gatekeepers and support us to use their premises, they did not seem interested in what we were doing in the workshops. Nonetheless, we reflected on whether we were (inadvertently) setting parents up to challenge the school's agenda, through encouraging parents to pursue different ways of thinking about maths that was not about directly working in service of the curriculum. Our projects highlighted that parents' expectations of home-based activity are that it is in service of the school agenda. Schools have specific ways of working with parents and children, which are usually school-directed. The Everyday Maths project, however, introduced parents to other ways of engaging in education. We encouraged parents and children to place less emphasis on homework and curriculum and to think about learning in more opportunistic, open-ended and exploratory ways. We justified our approach by highlighting the research evidence that homework rarely has a significant impact on attainment, and where it does, it serves to magnify the differences between pupils from more and less advantaged backgrounds.

Once the Everyday Maths workshops had been completed, we were invited by one of schools to do a one-off workshop with parents during their maths week. We were not quite sure what the school was expecting, but our workshop fitted with the theme and was a way of bringing parents into school. Attempting to run a one-off session demonstrated that what we were trying to do was complex and difficult: we could not expect to change parents' framing of what mathematical thinking is in just one 90-minute session. The limits of one workshop enabled us to demonstrate that there were other ways of thinking about mathematics, beyond the school curriculum. Supporting parents to try those alternative ways of thinking, and to explore how they could use that in conversations with their children, requires time and relationships and trust – we could not do this in a single session. The same applies to our work with teachers: our perspective required a significant shift for teachers, from ways of thinking about mathematics that were familiar to them (and necessary for them to do their jobs). This points to the radical, disruptive focus of Everyday Maths.

We needed to consider, then, whether we could realistically expect schools to interact in different ways with parents around their children's learning, and for parents to change their expectations around interactions with school. It was possible that our work could lead to parents feeling that they receive mixed messages from schools and from our work, about ways of supporting their children. The potential for the Everyday Maths project to disrupt relationships between parents and school is not something to be taken lightly. It is a tall order to expect schools to step aside from their curricular agenda in some interactions with parents, but not in others. Some schools are able to work in this way and successfully engage with parents, in ways that value parents' expertise and empower them (e.g. Hughes & Greenhough, 2011). For some schools, however, this may be more challenging (Haines Lyon, 2022). This of course raises questions about how we, as researchers, are positioning schools, and the extent to which we may or may not be potentially disruptive to their way of working. We need to remember, given the unpredictable nature of the parent workshops in Everyday Maths, we can't say for sure just how disruptive it will be.

Whose Agenda? Reflections on Participation in the Research Process

In discussions about our research, the question arose of whose agenda we were serving: we reflected on who it was that wrote the story of our research. In our research, we (as researchers) steered the course of the projects. This lead position should not be assumed by default (Areljung et al., 2021), and we made a conscious choice that we would make the decisions about the direction of our project. The agenda wasn't fixed, but the path it took was determined by what we felt was appropriate, given what we understood about our participants needs, wants and characteristics. The balance of power in our research was relatively asymmetrical (Areljung et al., 2021) – when considering how egalitarian our methods were (Brown, 2022), it was clear that we as researchers owned the research project. Sometimes in educational research this is implicit, but for us – because we were reflecting deeply on our methods and how to articulate them – our ownership was more explicit. The concept of participants as 'knowers' in research (Areljung et al., 2021) is helpful here: we positioned parents as 'knowers' of their lives, but we were the 'knowers' of the research process, and we could recognise the mathematical thinking that was inherent in their lives when they explained their everyday activity to us. Our role was, to some extent, to support parents to become 'knowers' – or rather 'recognisers or explorers' about the mathematics in their lives. As time went on, we wanted parents to be less focussed on being 'knowers' of mathematical knowledge, we wanted them to be happy to explore ideas. We held power, then, in terms of deciding that the participants should share their perspective, and in positioning their experiences as important (McGarry, 2016). Our power revealed itself in other ways too – we decided what actions we would and would not take, we decided where the research happened and its focus, and what the interactions between us and the participants were. We sought to influence our participants, and it was clear that this was not symmetrical. Of course, as researchers our actions and control of the project are also bound by ethics, but the same does not apply to our participants' actions.

Looking back, it is interesting to reflect on how explicitly we shared our thinking about the research process with our participants, and with Schools and funders as other stakeholders. We were positioning ourselves as 'experts' in the research process. This process was emergent and we were to some extent learning as we went along, but we drew on our previous research experience to help us negotiate the uncertainty. We discussed our plans for next steps with our participants as we went through the project, but were not explicit in terms of just how emergent the project was. While we wanted our participants to have some level of agency in our research, the process was not participatory. For us, the challenges around design – understanding what is ethical and realistic in terms of data production and analysis (as discussed by Pole et al., 1999) in the context of the overall aims and timescale of our research – did not lead us to working with a more participatory approach.

In the Everyday Maths project we created a toolkit for schools and parents, as discussed above. This was supposed to share a (very simplified) explanation of our process with suggestions for how schools could run the workshops themselves, and to support parents with their everyday maths practices. We tried to engage parents in creating this, but only a few chose to become involved. It is likely that there was no clear benefit to parents in this activity: we had to do this as a commitment to our funder, but essentially the project had been steered by us and to get parents involved and agentic in leading activity at this late stage was probably unrealistic. It is likely that the challenges we faced in supporting parents to shift their levels of agency throughout different stages of the project extended to creation of dissemination materials. It is clear to us now that working with dynamic levels of agency within a project requires very careful management, but this only became evident with hindsight.

It is helpful to unpick further how our expertise as researchers shaped the project – given that to some extent, we shaped both our expertise and the project as we went along. As researchers, we decide on concepts that we will work with, and the methods that are appropriate to use. Edwards and Fowler (2007) conceptualise 'intellectual technologies' and reflect on the implications of choices to use certain concepts in certain ways. Some of this work is around clearly defining what we are looking at – ideas or concepts that already exist and we put boundaries around, and label in a certain way – and some of this is about doing some thinking to come up with new ideas. We had to define what we meant by 'Everyday Maths'. The practice of everyday maths in itself is not new. The process of thinking, the intellectual work that we put into coming up with the term and defining what it was and what it was not, however, was important. Outlining the boundaries of everyday maths helped us think further about what the practice involved, it helped us reflect on how to access the actions involved in 'doing' everyday maths. We knew it was 'not school maths' – it was not structured, concept-led mathematics as delivered through the curriculum. Recognising this caused us to consider the boundary between school maths and everyday maths. As Edwards and Fowler (2007) discuss, intellectual technology can act as a shorthand once concepts are established and defined, but the work of defining that shorthand and delineating the boundaries of the concepts can also be useful.

This work of defining our concepts of course relates to our methods: what data we believe to be valuable, how we collect and analyse them, what claims we make and how our research impacts on others. What we call 'research methods' is actually a process (Netolicky & Barnes, 2018). 'Methods' are a series of decisions that flex and change as research progresses. The process goes beyond design, data collection and analysis: it also incorporates communication of the research and continued development of ideas and refining of those intellectual technologies. For us, this has happened through our subsequent discussions with parents and teachers, with other academics, through conference papers, journal articles, book chapters and now this book. Our expertise has shaped the projects, but the projects have also shaped our expertise as we use and shape our intellectual technologies.

The framing of our research – conceptually and methodologically – and how we communicate that impacts how others engage with it. Our findings are not clearly bound only to the data we collected. Our thinking has developed further following the engagement and responses of others as we shared our research findings (Chapter 10 will pick up on this). In the ongoing work of sharing our research, the boundary between school maths and everyday maths became very relevant and important – and we would not have been able to write this book in the years immediately following the projects' funded duration. Sharing and discussing and reframing our research, understanding what it means to others, how they interpret it and see its relevance, has helped us develop our own thinking and further refine our intellectual technologies. This relates to Edwards' (2011) concept of relational agency: the interaction between us as individual researchers, and between us as researchers and other stakeholders (such as teachers, parents and funders) of our research was important in shifting our thinking further. Netolicky and Barnes (2018) describe this as a Bakhtinian way of thinking (Bakhtin, 1981), where meaning is made through dialogue in a context. In this dialogue, different people have different roles and bring different perspectives. For us, this dialogue has been (and continues to be) crucial for the development of our ideas. Our research process goes far beyond a neatly packaged process of design, data collection and analysis, and reporting: we have taken the luxury of time, and using principles of slow research (Costas Batlle et al., 2022) has allowed us to discuss, reflect and develop our ideas further.

Intervention or Research? Packaging Our Process

In this book we have considered at length the impact of our research on others, especially our participants. Given that we were aiming to effect change in our participants' lives (in terms of their recognition and use of everyday maths to support learning conversations) and that we wanted to understand that change, our projects can be seen as interventions. These interventions, as discussed above, were emergent in their design and were focussed on both action and knowledge production. Although these characteristics are often found in participatory research (Brown, 2022), our research was led by us as researchers. Brown (2022) highlights the many aspects of research that participants can contribute to, including developing of research questions, developing the research approach and design, data collection, generation and analysis, and dissemination. While *our* approaches to these aspects were responsive to participants, ultimately our participants did not have a say in how these things were done. We led the research agenda, we didn't always lead the conversations themselves – but our stepping back to encourage participants to take the lead was not something that we overtly drew attention to. Importantly, we had the power in deciding when and how far we would step back and let participants take the lead.

Reflecting on insider/outsider relationships within the Everyday Maths project can help us further understand the nature of our research. We each were positioned differently within the project: there are many aspects of being insider and outsider, and for us, there were some ways in which we were 'like' our participants, and other ways in which we were different (Dhillon & Thomas, 2019). The most obvious comparison perhaps was related to parenthood (Ben and Tim were parents, Jo was not). Others, however, included our confidence in maths, the age of Ben's and Tim's children, the way we grappled with and experimented with ideas and new ways of thinking, how we spent our free time. Insiderness, however, is both about how we see ourselves and how we position ourselves in relation to the research, but also about how others see us (Floyd & Arthur, 2012). We shared some of the same experiences with our participants, but were in many respects still outsiders: we were not part of their school's parent community, we had a researcher role, we were 'from the University'. Our insiderness was not extensive or particularly deep, but we used it to help develop relationships and encourage an atmosphere of mutual trust.

This raises issues around relational responsibility. We were outsiders, and the process of trying to build trust meant that we impacted on relationships within the parent group and between parents and schools as the projects progressed. This was inevitable (Jay & Laing, 2022). To assume that the impact of research on participants and their relationships is always positive is somewhat presumptuous: there will be unintended consequences which we need to be mindful of. To try to mitigate against all of these, however, is unwise and will likely lead to bland research that does not effect change. As researchers, we should recognise the potential power of relationships and use that relational power responsibly.

Part of this power lies around how we persuade and encourage people to participate and ensure that participation remains a positive experience. Given that research can impact on participants in different ways as it progresses, we need to manage ongoing consent (DePalma, 2010) so that participants feel able to choose to continue working with us or not. Pre-emptive consent can be problematic when neither researchers nor participants know how the research will pan out (Nairn et al., 2020). Pre-emptive consent of course has a role to play in terms of awareness of the project and its potential for disruption, but with projects that take shape as they progress, consent should not just be a one-off exercise. The ethical governance required by institutions (which often includes pre-prepared information sheets and consent forms for participants) poses challenges for researchers using less structured, more emergent methods (Nairn et al., 2020). Working with principles of ongoing consent can feel more sympathetic and relational and was more aligned to our approach to the projects.

Our two projects raised different questions about the extent to which participants made active choices to participate, or whether their participation was more about a passive acceptance of participation. This distinction was highlighted by Nairn et al. (2020) and can be aligned to principles of sexual consent where making active choices to participate can be seen as genuine consent, but simply going along with someone else's motivation is not consent in its true form. In the Everyday Maths project, the workshops required parents to make an active decision to attend, to go somewhere different to where they would usually be. This meant that we were confident in claiming that participants were making an active choice – they were 'opting in' to our research. In addition, some parents chose not to attend after the first session, which again indicates that they felt able to decline the request for participation. Considering motivation for participation takes us back to our uncertainty about how the project would develop. This raises questions about what participants hoped to get out of the project, and whether that was a reasonable expectation. We assumed that parents were motivated to seek ways to develop their children's learning and hoped that we could help them explore that. But this again returns to our hope that the project would lead to some kind of change, but we were not sure how that change would happen, and what the exact nature and extent of that change would be. Of course, the parents who chose to participate throughout the project were the ones who shaped our thinking the most – those who did not participate, or dropped out early on were less influential in the development of our ideas. This participation bias is not unusual (Rönkä et al., 2014) and takes us back to the claim that the Everyday Maths project developed the way it did because of the individuals involved. The nature and extent of change and disruption, and the subsequent impact on our understanding of and ideas about the field, was tied in with the nature of the individuals involved in the project.

In summary, then, the Everyday Maths project involved working with relationships to effect change in the way parents thought about everyday maths. Subsequently, our role as researchers entailed us trying to understand that process. The workshops can be positioned as an intervention to support parents to recognise, to think about and talk about everyday maths. The research element entailed us working to understand that process: whether it was possible, how it was possible, how and why it happened in the way that it did. The intervention, then, was necessary to make the research happen: yet we didn't position the research as an intervention at the time. This is important, though, when we think about the potential for disruption. In education it can be hard to draw the line between practice and research, as DePalma (2010) points out. This means that there are unknown risks for participants when researchers seek to effect change. It is reasonable to expect research to pursue a broad agenda, but also (especially with research that is more emergent or participatory) to be able to pursue potentially positive consequences when the research takes an unexpected turn (Mearns et al., 2014). This takes research like ours a step away from a standard intervention, which is delineated in terms of expectations about actions and outcomes.

In our research, this sense of agency was important to the success of the projects: both projects were exploratory and shaped by us as we went along. Had we held less experience in research, this uncertainty would have presented more of a challenge: we would have been less confident to recognise and take opportunities to take the research in particular directions. Our research experience gave us a base from which to think through the ethical issues surrounding potential consequences and disruptive influence of our work: we needed to be able to both think things through before they happened and to work with complexities and respond when they arose. When involved in the day-to-day process of research projects (especially when working with lots of different schools), it can be easy to focus more on the activity and less on the broader agenda and bigger picture of purpose and consequences. Keeping a space within research to discuss and pursue the bigger agenda is, then, crucial (DePalma, 2010).

Disruption as Progress

Our discussion so far has largely centred around the way in which we influenced the direction of the project and the potential impact of that on our participants. There is, however, more to this theme of influence and disruption. Our projects also changed us, as researchers, as we progressed through the research. The projects changed the way we think about and see the world. Our research, then, was disruptive in many ways: for us, for our participants, and potentially for schools. This helps us to recognise that disruption can be a good thing, it can change the status quo. The purpose of academic research is often to further our understanding of a topic, and potentially change the way we think about what we are researching. Some disruption, then, is of course expected (why else would we do research?). Other unexpected or unintended disruptions might also arise from research, such as intellectual, relational/interactional or systemic disruptions. This meant that our role as researchers was difficult to articulate to schools and parents (and, at times, to ourselves): we did not know what disruption we would create, so it was hard to explain what we were trying to do, how we were facilitating the sessions and how we would make use of our research. As researchers we need to be mindful of this potential and intention for change and disruption.

Research like ours, that is centred around intervention, seeks to cause disruption. We have a responsibility to ensure that this is positive disruption and we think through potential consequences of our actions – even though the pathway and potential impact of the research is to some extent emergent. This is not necessarily about containing the disruption. We would like our research to have implications that reach beyond the impact on families' conceptual engagement with the maths they use in their everyday lives. We hope that our research will help families to think beyond curriculum boundaries, to reframe learning conversations that children have with their parents and with each other, and more broadly, to change families' relationships with learning. Additionally, we hope that schools may reflect on how they interact with parents. This is something that our research may influence and even initiate, but we cannot control how this plays out (like throwing a stone into a pond and the ripples travelling outwards). This is partly because our process is not tightly structured or clearly defined, so the impacts of what we do cannot be predicted and will vary widely according to context. It is also partly because our research is so dependent on relational dynamics, so the impact will also depend on the interactions between those involved. If our research was more straightforward and easier to package, and less dependent on relational dynamics, then it may have been easier to communicate the process more widely and thus more likely to be picked up by schools. We had lots of discussions about 'making the Everyday Maths workshops sustainable' without us leading them, yet to package them for others to run would ultimately change and maybe dilute the relational aspects that made them what they were. This highlights a trade-off between the extent of potential change for participants (where highly relational projects are likely to be more disruptive for those involved), and the reach of potential change in terms of rolling out the project more widely.

How, then, did we manage this responsibly? We aimed to support participants to feel comfortable sharing their thinking with us and with each other, so that the conversations they (and we) had had the potential to lead to change. The research context became a site in which all participants could be supported to progress their thinking, and contribute to the direction of the research, rather than just a place to exchange views. Participants fed into our research and helped to shape the context in which we were researching, but as McGarry (2016) outlines, researcher interpretations of participant voice play an important role. As researchers, part of our specialist skill is being able to translate 'voice' into something that can make change happen.

This again highlights the role of relational agency in this kind of research, as it explains how interactions between different individuals can lead to shifts in future thinking and behaviour (Edwards & Mackenzie, 2005). Working in this way involves integrating others' ideas with your own existing perspectives: relational agency is about how interactions with others change your ways of thinking and seeing the world. This was (in part, at least) how we intended disruption to happen. Given our background as interdisciplinary researchers, this way of working is familiar to us: it is part of the way that academic knowledge is produced. For our participants, however, the integration of others' ideas into their existing thinking and thus changing their ways of thinking is potentially an unfamiliar process. We hoped that parents in the Everyday Maths project would engage with us and with each other in this way, and that they would engage with their children in this way too. We hoped they would build relational agency, so that they could work with each other and with their children, to develop and change their ways of seeing the world together. We did not, however, explicitly explore this process with our participants – this is something that we came to understand through subsequent reflection on the process and so we do not know whether participants understand this as a part of the research process.

Our skills as researchers enabled us to grapple with and begin to understand the complexity of the research context. These research skills, though, take time to develop: to share them with participants over the relatively short duration of the workshops would be impossible. Researchers are often trained (be that implicitly or explicitly) in the process of learning new research skills. For participants with little or no history of conducting research, learning research skills and principles is likely to be unfamiliar and possibly difficult. The extent to which participants have the time and resource, as well as the required levels of understanding, to engage in the complexity of the research process (Mearns et al., 2014) will further impact on the potential for change and disruption. The boundaries that shape participation may determine that all participants *can* do is respond to the researcher agenda and this limits the change and disruption that can take place.

The Potential for Change

Our projects aimed to demonstrate that there is a multiplicity of activity that can be used as a foundation for mathematical conversations, and this can be accessed by all families no matter what their background. This can start to even out the differences between families that are highlighted by the school curriculum and homework, which often works in favour of already advantaged families (Fitzmaurice et al., 2021; Lutz & Jayaram, 2015). It is unrealistic, however, to expect teachers to bring together the different family experiences of all 30 or more children in their class to develop a shared, coherent and predictable learning opportunity. We proposed that it was appropriate for home learning to be different to classroom learning: families are able to explore ideas in their own way, but schools cannot do so because of the need for a coherent curriculum. Our work in the Everyday Maths project was about empowering parents to recognise the opportunities that arose in family life, and giving them the confidence to use those opportunities.

In doing this, we were aware of the potential for parents to feel that we were undermining the school agenda. In parental engagement work, schools often position parents as acting in service of the school's performativity agenda. This can cause frustration and anxiety for parents who may not be familiar with the school curriculum, and do not know how to act as teachers (Jay et al., 2018). Our approach was to highlight *other* things that families could do, that would still be helpful but were not necessarily directly relevant to the school curriculum. We were not saying that the school agenda didn't matter, but we aimed to empower parents to step away from the idea that the only way to help their child's learning is by directly following the school curriculum. This meant that we were potentially disrupting the balance of existing school/parent relationships. Parents had their own expectations of how the curriculum works, around 'right' answers to questions and around curriculum boundaries. These ideas link closely to the school performativity agenda as they are the foundations of much of the assessment that happens in classrooms. As discussed in previous chapters, asking parents (and potentially teachers, if they were to run the workshops) to step away from this and instead discuss ideas without a focus on correct answers, was hard for many parents and for teachers too. Our agenda was more focussed on having interesting conversations – yet this is a big jump for both schools and many parents in terms of how they think about learning.

In the early days of trying to share the findings of our research and encourage schools to take forward the ideas from the Everyday Maths project, we came to recognise the struggle that schools would face in trying to shift the school/parent relationship. Schools are used to leading in these relationships. They are in a powerful position and hold expert knowledge about curriculum. Parents and pupils expect schools to hold this expertise, so it is very easy for schools to work in this way. For schools to step away from being powerful, and for parents to feel comfortable in reshaping their relationships with schools is ambitious and potentially extremely disruptive. We encouraged parents to work in ways that were not in direct service to the school agenda and to reframe how they thought about their roles in their child's learning. We needed to pay careful attention to our implicit messaging about how we positioned schools and consider whether empowering parents to focus on family activity rather than the school curriculum would fit in with how schools want parents to behave (Goodall, 2017; Goodall & Montgomery, 2013; Harris & Goodall, 2008).

Our Everyday Maths project aimed to empower parents, but in doing so were we disempowering the school? This was – and is – a tricky line to tread, but one that is important to pay attention to because it has the potential to disrupt relationships between schools and parents, and ultimately between the schools and the researcher community. Our projects took as a starting point the power imbalance between schools and families, where schools act as the leaders in learning, and families (parents and children) as followers. We sought to reposition families as leaders in an aspect of learning. Our research went some way beyond understanding what is happening, to intervening. In the Everyday Maths project, we tried to change parents' understanding of what mathematical thinking entailed and subsequently how they interacted with their children about maths. We were open about our agenda, but we were not sure whether it would be successful or have an impact. Some participants appeared to develop a new way of framing mathematics and change how they approached family learning. In doing this, we were not actively trying to disrupt the home/school relationship, yet problem-atising this relationship was the starting point for our intervention. The question still remains, then, as to whether what we were doing was potentially also a positive disruption for schools.

Taking the ideas that we developed through the project, and sharing them in ways that were meaningful to schools and parents, presented a challenge. Our ideas and understanding about everyday maths came from a range of different sources: the data collection with participants did not directly result in a straightforward, coherent narrative about family learning. Some participants would recognise their words – and hopefully their thoughts and intentions – as we share our research outputs. Some may wonder how we had come to reach our conclusions. In communicating with parents and teachers individual stories can create resonance. We acknowledge this, but step beyond these individual stories to work at a more macro level. As researchers, we consider our data with different lenses and use that process to develop our understanding and ideas and to enable a step-change in how everyday maths is conceptualised and used. Of course we present this in different ways with different foci to different audiences – including parents, teachers, researchers and funders. Further, the way in which we have shared our understanding of everyday maths has changed over the years as our thinking has evolved and as we continue to discuss and reflect on the project. The way in which we are continuing to frame and reframe the findings from the project is part of the disruption that can – and should – be caused by research.

Chapter 10

Scaling Up the Everyday Maths Workshops

Scaling up the products of research is a major challenge in any area of education. On top of this, developing effective parental engagement interventions for mathematics learning presents particular challenges.

Huat See and Gorard (2015) have shown that many parental involvement and engagement interventions fail to show positive effects on learning. In fact, a good proportion of the higher quality evaluations that were included in their review showed negative effects. Having worked in this area for a number of years now, we believe there are three main reasons why interventions often don't work in the way they are intended to work.

- Developers and teachers underestimate the amount of time required to develop positive relationships with parents, carers and families if these are not already in place.
- Interventions often ask parents and carers to lead activities that are too close to children's classroom experience.
- Interventions are often too narrow in focus – for example, training parents to carry out a particular set of arithmetic operations. This means that changes in parents' behaviours are necessarily short term, as when children move onto other content parents require further training.

The workshops developed during the Everyday Maths project address these three issues directly. They focus on relationship-building before mathematics learning, they encourage activity that is complementary to classroom learning rather than replicating it and they are broad in focus. Our evaluation of the workshops led us to believe that it would be useful to scale up the workshops to reach larger numbers of parents, carers and children. However, there were still some tricky hurdles to clear before such scaling up could begin.

Much of the work carried out under the banner of 'translational research' in education comprises the dissemination of information. While this is perhaps an important component of our work as researchers, we argue that on its own it is unlikely to change practice in a substantial way. This is because making use of research outputs through development of practice in the classroom involves knowing more than the fact that the research exists, or what the research says

Parental Engagement and Out-of-School Mathematics Learning, 123–134
Copyright © 2023 Tim Jay and Jo Rose
Published under exclusive licence by Emerald Publishing Limited
doi:10.1108/978-1-78769-705-820231010

about some aspect of teaching and learning. Work is generally required to *translate* findings and outputs from research so that they can be used effectively by teachers in classrooms. This is because there are substantial differences between the implementation of an intervention that is part of a research project and the implementation of an intervention as part of teaching practice. A summary of key differences is shown in Table 1.

There are a few aspects of Table 2 that are worth elaborating on a little further here, which relate to specific qualities of the Everyday Maths workshops. Firstly, elaborating on the age of participants, the Everyday Maths research project was carried out with parents and carers with at least one child in Year 3 at primary school (children aged seven to eight years old). However, as we will see later in this chapter, feedback from teachers at an early stage in scaling up told us that it could be better to focus on children in Reception year (four to five-year-olds). While this did not require any changes to the main principles of the workshops, there were differences in the kinds of conversations and kinds of activities that parents were likely to engage in with their children.

A second area to elaborate on here a little further is the position of teachers as facilitators of the intervention. We have emphasised in earlier parts of this book that the Everyday Maths workshops are not about replicating classroom activity, but are about empowering parents and carers to consider themselves as experts in supporting their children's learning through conversations about everyday family life and activity. For some teachers this can represent a significant challenge, as it runs counter to the usual relationship between teacher and parents where the teacher is the expert and is the person who makes decisions about what and how children are learning.

Finally, levels of parental involvement and engagement vary considerably across schools. When our research team was working with schools during the development of the Everyday Maths workshops, we saw that some schools were in regular contact with most parents, while others rarely had contact. For example, some schools had the vast majority of parents attending parents' evenings, and some schools ran 'stay and play' events and similar where parents were invited into the classroom during the school day to take part in activities with their children. Other schools, though, did not regularly invite parents into the school and often saw low attendance at parents' evenings. Schools' current levels of parental involvement made a difference to the effort required to recruit parents to our workshops. Similarly, teachers considering using the Everyday Maths approach with families needed to consider the quality of existing relationships, as this would affect decisions about recruitment strategy.

Dissemination Does Not Necessarily Lead to Impact

Towards the end of the Everyday Maths research project, we worked hard to share the outcomes with various audiences including primary teachers and primary school mathematics leads. This involved presentations of the research at a number of events of different sizes. We were aware that a one-off presentation of an hour or so was too little to expect it to lead to changes in schools and in

Table 2. Differences Between Implementation of an Intervention as Part of a Research Project and as Part of Teaching Practice.

Factor	Implementation in a Research Project	Implementation in Teaching Practice
Time	Project planned from outset with time for researchers to carry out iterative cycle of design and evaluation.	Planning for implementation must be done within limited time, alongside existing work.
Resources	Project funding allows for development and production of resources that support the implementation of the intervention.	Limited budget available for production of resources, so if free resources are not available, this can be challenging.
Ages	Research projects often carried out with children in a narrow age range.	Teachers may be interested in applying research with a different age group from that with whom the research was conducted.
Group sizes	Project can be carried with a group size that is appropriate to the stage of the project or one that is convenient for the researcher.	It can be difficult for teachers to offer something to only a subset of the class and more likely that any intervention would need to be delivered to all children in the class.
Demographics	Researchers are likely to try and work with participants from diverse demographic groups (bearing in mind ethnicity, SES, gender, geographical location and so on), although there will be limitations due to sample size.	Teachers will have a group of children and families to work with that may or may not resemble the mix of participants in a research project. Differences in demographic variables may mean that adaptations may be needed.
Facilitator	The research team will often facilitate the intervention. They will have deep knowledge of the purpose and design of the intervention and will be highly motivated for it to be	The teacher will facilitate the intervention. They may know participants well, but may need time to develop knowledge and understanding of the design and purpose of the

Table 2. *(Continued)*

Factor	Implementation in a Research Project	Implementation in Teaching Practice
	successful (in whatever terms success has been defined for the project). However, they will not necessarily know the participants well.	intervention. They may have different criteria for 'success' than the research team.
Participant engagement	If participants are not highly engaged with the project, then an alternative group can be recruited at a later date.	The teacher has just one opportunity to engage participants (especially if the participant group is parents/carers) and does not have a backup group to go to if things go wrong.

teachers' practice. For this reason, we offered attendees at this session our support in implementing the Everyday Maths workshops in their schools if it was something they were interested in doing. While we do not believe that these presentations led to impact of any significance directly, we found that they did allow us to make contact with a group of teachers who were interested in working with us to improve parental engagement in mathematics learning in their schools.

Through teachers contacting us after presentations, we were able to work with a group of teachers in a diverse set of schools to support the use of the Everyday Maths workshops approach. In working with this group of teachers one-to-one, we were able to explore methods for implementing this approach in schools as well as challenges that needed to be addressed. This work was also a prompt for us to consult some of the literature outside of the education discipline on the translation of research to impact.

What Is Needed for Research to Impact on Practice?

As noted earlier in this chapter, work is needed to translate research findings so that they can be used in practice. However, there is little guidance in the educational research literature on how this can happen. 'Translational research' is often used to refer to the dissemination of research evidence in teacher-friendly formats, rather than to any more involved work to encourage change. For this reason, we draw on research from outside of the education discipline, where there is a longer history of this kind of work. In this section, we briefly introduce research from three key areas: medicine and public health, management and design. These areas have strongly influenced our thinking about how best to take research outputs to teachers and schools.

The View From Public Health

In public health research, authors refer to multiple 'translation gaps', and note that the use of the term 'translational research' to refer to more than one kind of gap has the potential to lead to some confusions (e.g. Woolf, 2008). Sung et al. (2003), reporting on a meeting of the Clinical Research Roundtable at the US Institute of Medicine, refer to 'T1' research as the translation of basic research to human studies, and 'T2' research as the translation of new knowledge into clinical practice and health decision-making. Sung et al. go on to argue that T1 research is relatively well-funded, and that researchers have good experience and training in conducting T1 research. However, T2 research is less well understood by researchers and has less attention from funders. There is a helpful analogy here with educational research. We might see T1 research in education as the creation and evaluation of prototypical resources, activities, or lesson plans, on the basis of research evidence. We would then see T2 research as the translation of evidence from such evaluations into the improvement of educational decision-making and children's learning at scale. In education, as in public health, there appears to be a relatively large amount of know-how, experience and funding available for T1 research, given these definitions, and relatively little for T2. While the Education Endowment Foundation in the United Kingdom, and funding bodies with similar missions elsewhere have funded large-scale randomised controlled trials (RCTs) of educational interventions, the actual methods of redesign and implementation of interventions at scale and methods of translation of evidence from trials to adoption in policy and practice have received little attention.

Public health researchers refer to the broad range of stakeholders that might benefit from the translation of research. Woolf et al. (2015, p. 466) list the following:

- People caring for their own health (or their caretakers), who can use research to make choices about healthy lifestyles, disease management and injury prevention.
- Clinicians, social workers, teachers and other service providers, who can use research to determine how best to care for patients/clients.
- Employers, who can implement policies to improve the health and safety of workers.
- Manufacturers, who can make products and services safer and more healthful for consumers.
- Urban planners and developers, who can modify the built environment to improve health and reduce harmful exposures.
- Community members and organisations, who can form coalitions for collective impact on health outcomes, including advocacy organisations, interest groups, coalitions, voluntary associations and non-profit organisations that represent the involved parties.
- Investors, community foundations and health plans, who can make investments to promote health and the social determinants of health.

– Elected officials and voters, who can enact legislation and invest in policies and programs that can improve public health.

An analogous list could be created for educational research, but the ambition to reach a similarly wide-ranging group of stakeholders in education is rarely seen.

The View From Management

We draw on a relatively well-developed research literature in change management – this has helped us to develop an understanding of tools and techniques that may be useful in fostering policy and practice changes in institutions like schools. As in the public health literature discussed above, in management research there is a recognition that:

- Good ideas with no ideas on how to implement them are wasted ideas.
- Change does not just happen but must be led.
- It is not only a matter of where to go but also how to get there (Mader et al., 2013).

We know from our own conversations with teachers and education leaders that there are teachers in schools that would like to improve levels of parental engagement. We also know that many teachers do not know what they can do to achieve such improvement, and that teachers also have concerns about potential risks involved in making changes to their ways of working with parents. It is clear that change does not happen without a plan – there must be a clear strategy for change and appropriate support for schools and teachers to change established ways of doing things.

Stanley (2006) sets out seven principles for effective change management in education. These principles focus primarily on the identification of suitable agents of change, on working to understand current practices, and on ways to communicate, and to recruit agents of change to support, strategy to implement change. These principles influenced our thinking about how to work with teachers to scale up the Everyday Maths workshops. In particular, we were aware that our work directly with parents had shown us that there is a wide variation in current levels of home–school communication, and also in teachers' experience and attitudes around working with parents. We were keen to be careful to avoid starting by telling teachers what they 'should' be doing, and instead to begin our work with teachers by exploring with them how they evaluated their current levels of communication and relationships with parents, where they felt there were opportunities for improvement and what they thought might be barriers to change. This initial work gave us a much better position to suggest strategy for change towards implementing the Everyday Maths workshop sessions – and a better sense of what foundational work in establishing positive home–school relationships might or might not be needed first.

The View From Design

Our thinking about how to translate our research into practice has been influenced by design-based research approaches in a number of important ways. One key principle we have drawn on is that research findings do not translate into impact unproblematically – good design is required for outcomes to be useable by other stakeholders (Design-Based Research Collective, 2003). We knew from our previous research that the Everyday Maths project approach worked well when we as a research team were facilitating workshops, but were also aware that this did not necessarily mean that the approach would work equally well when the workshops were facilitated by teachers.

A design research approach helped us in finding ways to translate the workshops from a research exercise facilitated by us as a research team, into a home–school-partnership initiative facilitated by teachers. 'In design-based research, practitioners and researchers work together to produce meaningful change in contexts of practice (e.g., classrooms, after-school programs, teacher on-line communities). Such collaboration means that goals and design constraints are drawn from the local context as well as the researcher's agenda' (Design-Based Research Collective, 2003, p. 6). To ensure that the workshops would work well for teachers in their own settings, we worked with groups of teachers following an iterative approach so that teachers could design and evaluate new ways of working with parents, based on the Everyday Maths project approach, in their own schools. We believed that this approach would have a better chance of success than taking a one-size-fits-all approach for all schools and teachers.

Co-design Workshops With Teachers

In our one-to-one work with teachers interested in implementing the Everyday Maths approach for parental engagement, we learnt a lot about the challenges involved and about ways to address these challenges. Together with our reading of previous research on translating research to practice, we felt that this put us in a stronger position to scale up our impact further. Two key issues that we learnt about from our initial work with teachers are detailed here:

Age of Children

In the original research project, we worked with parents and carers who had at least one child in Year 3 in primary school (aged seven–eight years). From our reading of the literature, we believed that this was an age where many parents and teachers started to feel that parental engagement was becoming more difficult, while at the same time the mathematics that children were learning at school was not out of the reach of most parents. However, for teachers introducing the workshop approach into their own schools, this was not always an ideal group to work with. In fact many teachers have preferred to introduce the workshops for parents of children in Reception year (aged four–five years). This allowed teachers and schools to build good connections with parents and families and to encourage good learning at home right from the beginning of children's time in a new school, rather than trying to 'fix' relationships and practices in Year 3.

Confidence and Experience of the Teacher

Teachers that we have worked with have varied in terms of the length of experience that they have as a teacher and in their confidence working with parents and in mathematics. Some teachers with less experience or confidence found some aspects of the workshop approach difficult to manage. Primarily, difficulties stemmed from the need to allow parents to be the experts in their children's out-of-school lives and in thinking about how to introduce mathematical ideas and language into everyday conversations. These teachers felt that they would be more comfortable with a more traditional, teacher-led, approach where they could be more directive and do more of the talking. This would be something that we needed to work on with teachers, so that they felt more comfortable with a new approach.

Further to these, we were keen to build on what we had learnt when working directly with children, and then with parents, to explore the mathematics everyday out-of-school lives. What was common to both of those areas of work was our commitment to treating participants as experts in their context, while support them to explore an unfamiliar approach to activity. Our experience of facilitating these previous projects with children and with parents showed us that the process of attending to and elaborating on their strengths and expertise at the beginning of a project was a fundamental ingredient needed to empower participants to take a potentially risky step into unfamiliar territory. We planned to take the same approach with teachers – beginning by attending to and building on their expertise in managing learning in the classroom, and then using this as a safe place from which to take a risky step towards working with parents in a new way.

Our approach to working with each group – children, parents and teachers – can be seen as following many aspects of a therapeutic approach. Essentially, we saw our role as facilitators not as teaching our participants how to do something new but as supporting our participants to reveal to themselves something that they already knew but were preventing themselves from putting into action due to various barriers. For parents, we have already discussed some of the major barriers – for example:

(1) Being constrained by curriculum boundaries, i.e. believing that if a conversation is to support mathematics learning, then it should not be about some other curriculum subject (e.g. science, history, geography) as well
(2) Thinking that mathematical conversations needed to end up with a 'right answer'
(3) Thinking that mathematics at home should always resemble mathematics in classrooms

These barriers prevent parents from engaging in meaningful interactions about mathematics with their children that have potential for supporting learning. The development and evaluation of the Everyday Maths workshops helped show that these barriers could be addressed, and once they were addressed, that parents could experience dramatic increases in the quantity and quality of mathematical interactions at home.

In preparing to work with teachers, we anticipated a similar set of barriers – comprising preconceptions about how teachers should work with parents around parental engagement in learning that constrained the kind of activity and interaction that might be possible. Some were the same for both groups, including thinking that mathematics at home should always resemble mathematics in classrooms. We know that it is fairly common practice for schools to organise workshops where parents are shown how children are being taught various arithmetic operations, for example, so that they can support children to carry out these operations at home. Similarly, we anticipated that teachers may have preconceptions about what 'counts' as mathematics in everyday life and may be overly constrained by their understanding of the national curriculum. However, we were also open to learning more about further potential barriers as our work with teachers progressed.

Workshops With Teachers

We drew on some of the principles of design research as discussed above in planning our work with teachers. The 'Analyse, Design, Implement, Evaluate' cycle was used as a way to structure a set of workshop sessions with teachers. We also primed teachers with the idea that we would support them through the first design cycle, but that they should plan for further cycles to refine their thinking and practice around parental engagement after our work with them was over.

Analyse

In our first session with teachers, we shared our knowledge and understanding of some of the research on parental engagement, highlighting the benefits of good parental engagement in mathematics learning at home as well as some of the difficulties in implementing effective parental engagement interventions in schools. We then encouraged teachers to consider their current relationships with the parents of children in their classes and to think about what they already knew or suspected about levels of parental engagement in children's mathematics learning in children's homes. Teachers' 'homework' after this session was to carry out some data collection to further develop their understanding of their starting point for improving parental engagement in their schools. The majority of teachers used a brief survey to collect data on parents' behaviours and attitudes around their children's mathematics learning for this part of the project.

Design

In the second session, we supported teachers to plan activities for parents based on those that we designed and carried out during the Everyday Maths project. We encouraged teachers to adapt the sessions in whatever ways that they felt were needed in order to fit the needs of both themselves and their approaches to teaching, and according to the current status of their relationships with parents of children in their classes and current attitudes of parents to mathematics learning, based on data that they had collected since the last session. During this session we were careful to bear in mind guidance from the Design-Based Research Collective (2002), that in working with teachers to adapt the Everyday Maths materials to their circumstances we had to distinguish between a 'lethal mutation' (Brown & Campione, 1996) – a reinterpretation that no longer captures the pedagogical essence of the innovation – from a productive adaptation – a reinterpretation that preserves this essence but tailors the activity to the needs and characteristics of particular groups.

Implement and Evaluate

We supported teachers to create an evaluation plan for their interventions with parents. For the design cycle to function effectively, teachers needed to collect data that could tell them whether their work with parents had led to changes that they were aiming for and could provide some hints as to how the activities could be improved for the future. Teachers not only often repeated the survey used in the 'Analyse' phase but also supplemented this with informal conversation with parents, and their own observations of the workshops, of interactions between parents and of children in their classrooms during and after sessions with parents.

Outcomes From the Teacher Workshops

All of the teachers who attended the first workshop continued to attend all workshops throughout the project, which we interpreted very positively. All of the teachers who participated in the project also carried out parental engagement interventions, based on the Everyday Maths project approach, with parents in their schools.

Teachers all reported positive changes in their own evaluations of parental engagement. Surveys carried out by teachers, for example, showed higher levels of interactions involving mathematics and confidence in supporting children's mathematics learning, after the workshops relative to before. However, teachers were often more persuaded by changes that they saw in children's behaviours and attitudes around mathematics learning in classrooms. Teachers commented on particular children who they had previously judged to have low levels of confidence and engagement in mathematics in the classroom as having changed significantly following their parents' involvement in interventions at that school.

One question for further research concerns the likely mechanism(s) for changes in children's behaviours and attitudes following interventions like these. We believe that at least some of these positive changes will be due to the increased quantity and quality of parents' interactions with children that involve mathematical language and concepts. The increased frequency and quality of these interactions at home are likely to improve children's receptivity to similar interactions in the classroom and improve their engagement and interest in mathematical concepts and language more generally. However, it is also possible that participation in this project encouraged teachers to think differently about low levels of interest, engagement or confidence in mathematics in the classroom and to consider new ways in which the teachers themselves could draw on everyday activities to spark mathematical conversations with children. Teasing apart such potential mechanisms could certainly be a challenge. It is possible that it would be better to be content that there are positive outcomes, regardless of the mechanism for their realisation.

Challenges and Next Steps in Scaling Up

Further research is needed in a number of key areas, in order to make the case for change in practice more widely than we have been able to achieve to date. One area where more data would be useful is in tracking effects on children's learning due to their parents' participation in the workshops. So far, we have data from parents and from teachers that tell us that the workshops have value – and these data include reports of perceived improvements in children's learning and in children's attitudes to mathematics. However, we do not yet have direct evidence that the workshops have led to measurable changes in children's performance in mathematics classrooms. In the current climate, this could be considered key to wider take-up of our approach in schools. Evaluating any changes in children's learning outcomes that are due to their parents' participation in activities such as the Everyday Maths workshops would represent a major challenge, however. A key challenge for this kind of evaluation would be the amount of time likely required to go from work with teachers, through to teachers' work with parents, through to parents' conversation with children, and finally to improvements in children's thinking and learning about mathematics. Criticism has been level at the use of RCTs of educational interventions for a number of reasons, including the fact that interventions are often trialled on too short a timescale to expect a trial to show effectiveness (Rossi et al., 1999; Ginsburg & Smith, 2016). For example, Ginsburg and Smith suggest that it can take two or three years for a complex intervention to be reliably implemented. A second challenge for this kind of evaluation of the Everyday Maths workshops is the fact that by their nature and design, their implementation will be different in each school as discussed in previous chapters. Depending on teachers' initial relationships with parents, parents' current levels of knowledge, confidence and activity with regard to mathematics at home, and current school approaches for parental engagement and home–school communication, different form of implementation of the Everyday Maths workshops will be needed, and more or less preparation will be required for that implementation. This can make it complex to determine what it is exactly about the intervention that is being trialled, and following this, to generate measures of 'fidelity' to show how well the intervention has been implemented in different contexts.

If the nature of the Everyday Maths workshops does not align well with an RCT evaluation approach, then we need to think about alternatives. We believe that a 'slow burn' approach is more suitable for the kind of change in relation-ships and processes that these workshops involve. To date, schools' and teachers' use of the Everyday Maths workshops in schools has spread due to word of mouth. Initially, this has been through discussions between members of our research team and teachers in schools, but as teachers have used the workshops and adapted them to their settings, they have shared their experiences with other teachers. Spread of the use of the Everyday Maths workshops has been supported by professional development networks that teachers are engaged with, including the regional Maths Hubs, for example.[1]

Some of the key challenges that we have grappled with in scaling up across schools have been very similar to those that we have worked with parents and teachers on within schools. For example, it has been challenging to work with schools that are too attached to traditional homework or to adherence to a strictly defined and boundaried mathematics curriculum, for example. For teachers to use the Everyday Maths workshop approach effectively in their schools, they have needed to have the confidence to allow and support parents to be creative in their own ways of bringing out mathematical talk in their everyday lives. As discussed previously in the book, this requires a certain level of trust on both teachers' and parents' part to work well. However, despite some challenges in taking this approach to schools, we continue to receive positive reports from teachers where improved mathematics talk at home has changed the ways that children engage with mathematics in the classroom.

---

[1]https://www.ncetm.org.uk/maths-hubs/

Chapter 11

Concluding Reflections

The usual approach to publishing and disseminating academic research is through series of relatively brief articles in academic journals. The usual format and style of journal articles strongly encourages a tight focus on a small number of research questions that address a particular aspect of an issue. This compartmentalisation of big questions into concise packaged articles is something that we were reacting against when we decided to start writing this book. While it is possible to write articles about various aspects of children's out-of-school mathematics learning, we feel that this research is fundamentally entwined with the methodological, theoretical, political and practical issues that we have had the space to explore further in this book. We have enjoyed taking the time to engage in depth with some of these issues and to consider how they relate with each other in the conduct of research on out-of-school learning of mathematics. This process has prompted some reflection on what this means in interpreting our own research and what it means for continued work in this field. In this concluding chapter, we explore three of our reflections on the book as a whole and consider how these might inform future work.

In this book we have tried to develop some of the cross-cutting themes in our research on parental engagement and out-of-school learning in mathematics, and to develop some of the connections amongst them. We have included chapters on the different perceived purposes of education that various parties bring to the conversation, and the related expectations that these perceived purposes bring about in relation to participation in research in this field. Due to these different perceived purposes and expectations, we have seen that careful work is required in order to engage various groups with research and that different strategies are likely to need to be brought to bear for different groups and individuals. We have discussed issues around the uncertainty that different parties involved in the research may experience when exploring new potential sites of, and approaches to, learning, or when trying out a novel intervention. In relation to this uncertainty, we have considered the effects and associated ethical implications of disruption to normal practices on school and family life. What links these issues together is the fact that research on out-of-school learning necessarily involves consideration of the interplay among different groups. Further to this, we have seen that consideration of such interplay and relationships between groups is also

Parental Engagement and Out-of-School Mathematics Learning, 135–137
Copyright © 2023 Tim Jay and Jo Rose
Published under exclusive licence by Emerald Publishing Limited
doi:10.1108/978-1-78769-705-820231011

in thinking about how to best support children's learning. We argue that our research shows that high-quality learning depends on a community approach, with schools, teachers, families and children and young people working in concert on shared goals with a shared approach. However, what we tend to see in practice, in the United Kingdom at least, is an overly school-centred approach with limited communication amongst groups. We hope that our research can prompt further research and development in this area, and long-term help lead to improved community approaches to education.

The second main area of reflection for us is on the 'deconstruction' of home and school with regard to children's learning. Related to the paragraph above, here we think about the balance of attention and resource given to the learning that takes place in school, as opposed to the learning that takes places outside of school. We have seen that, across the studies that we have discussed in this book, without intervention, there is very little attention given by teachers and parents to any learning that takes place outside of school. This is a state of affairs that has clearly evolved over many years, but when re-examined given what we now know about out-of-school learning seems at odds with the breadth of backgrounds, interests and future ambitions that children and young people bring to their learning. We have seen throughout this book that families are able to support children to make connections between the classroom and everyday life in a way that teachers in schools cannot. We argue also that, as a primary purpose of education is to prepare children for future life and work, some additional focus on children's learning outside of school is needed to support learners' ability to apply what they have learnt in the classroom in situations outside the classroom. We hope that future research can continue to explore ways to support children and young people to use mathematics they experience in the classroom, and that they implicitly encounter in their everyday lives, in ways that improve their experience of life, learning and work. We further hope that such research can contribute to positive developments in parental engagement and community education to best support children's learning.

Finally, our third area of reflection here returns us to the 'breaking out of the boundaries' phrase in the title of the book. Throughout the book, we have seen variations of a phenomenon where teachers, families and children impose imaginary limits or rules on their understandings of concepts including 'mathematics' and 'learning'. We have also seen that when these groups are encouraged to examine such imaginary limits, it can become easier to create opportunities for mathematical thinking and learning. A great example of this was from a discussion between parents of what activities 'counted' as mathematical. For example – activities like swinging on a rope swing (is this mathematics or is it physics?), thinking about supply and demand (economics or mathematics?), thinking about route planning and travel (geography or mathematics?), or thinking about pattern and repetition (art or mathematics?). We saw how this kind of worry unnecessarily restricted parents' role in supporting children's mathematical thinking and learning. A broader definition of 'mathematics' – one that allowed overlap with other curriculum areas – allowed parents to think more creatively about creating opportunities for their children to engage with mathematical thinking. Similarly, definitions of 'mathematical thinking' that included features like 'always ends up with the one correct answer' restricted parents' thinking about how they could encourage use of mathematical language through use of open questions and creative play. We hope that the research presented in this book can support those with a focus on mathematics learning to reconsider any potentially unhelpful restrictions they may be placing on their definitions of 'mathematics' or of 'learning'.

This book will be useful for researchers, in terms of highlighting the complexity of research on informal learning, considering new ways of framing research problems in the field of learning and considering the different ways of building research relationships in this area. Educators might draw from this book in terms of considering the interactions between the different contexts of learning, reflecting on how children's lives beyond the curriculum can contribute to their understanding of topics and developing creative approaches to integrate everyday activity with existing formal teaching practices. We hope that this will also be of use to policymakers, through our foregrounding of learning beyond the classroom and curriculum and demonstrating the value of this in supporting the curriculum.

Writing this book has been transformational for us, as researchers and authors. It has made us more open in our research approaches and helped us to recognise the limits (as well as the value!) of more traditional educational research approaches. We have reflected on the level of control we can have in our research, and now believe that for more interesting or useful research findings, we need to be happy to relinquish control of process and outcomes. In the workshops with parents in the Everyday Maths project, we had to hold back and let parents take workshop in ways that felt appropriate for them. We used the same approach with teachers when scaling up, as detailed in Chapter 10: we couldn't tell teachers exactly what to and how to implement ideas in their own schools. They needed to work out how to use our ideas in their own ways, rather than us being overly prescriptive. In such work there is no perfect standardised outcome that we are looking for from the use of our ideas: in a sense the 'perfect' outcome is that each school or family uses our ideas in ways that are appropriate for them. This kind of research is context-dependent and shaped by the individuals involved with their many different lives, needs, wants and interests. We intend to take this exploratory, flexible approach into future research both in schools and beyond, beyond measurement and structure.

Through this book, we have contributed to understanding of how parents can be encouraged to engage in their children's learning through everyday activity, beyond school. Through our understanding of barriers to this, we have developed new insights about parental relationships with their children's learning. This has led us to propose a more parent-centred approach to promoting shared family learning activities and opportunities. From this, we now understand the importance of considering the quality – rather than the quantity – of learning interactions and activity.

References

Adu-Ampong, E. A., & Adams, E. A. (2020). "But you are also Ghanaian, you should know": Negotiating the insider–outsider research positionality in the fieldwork encounter. *Qualitative Inquiry, 26*(6), 583–592. https://doi.org/10.1177/1077800419846532

Akkerman, S., & Bakker, A. (2011). Boundary crossing and boundary objects. *Review of Educational Research, 81*(2), 132–169. https://doi.org/10.3102/0034654311404435

Altay, M., Yalvaç, B., & Yeltekin, E. (2017). 8th grade student's skill of connecting mathematics to real life. *Journal of Education and Training Studies, 5*(10), 158–166. https://doi.org/10.11114/jets.v5i10.2614

Anyon, J. (1980). Social class and the hidden curriculum of work. *Journal of Education, 162*(1), 67–92. https://doi.org/10.1177/002205748016200106

Areljung, S., Leden, L., & Wiblom, J. (2021). Expanding the notion of 'ownership' in participatory research involving teachers and researchers. *International Journal of Research and Method in Education, 44*(5), 463–473. https://doi.org/10.1080/1743727X.2021.1892060

Baker, D., & Street, B. (2004). Mathematics as social. *For the Learning of Mathematics, 24*(2), 19–21. https://www.jstor.org/stable/40248453

Baker, D., Street, B., & Tomlin, A. (2003). Mathematics as social: Understanding relationships between home and school numeracy practices. *For the Learning of Mathematics, 23*(3), 11–15. https://www.jstor.org/stable/40248453

Bakhtin, M. (1981). *The dialogic imagination: Four essays* (Vol. 1). University of Texas Press.

Bayeck, R. (2022, July). Positionality: The interplay of space, context and identity. *International Journal of Qualitative Methods, 21*, 1–9. https://doi.org/10.1177/16094069221114

Berger, R. (2015). Now I see it, now I don't: researcher's position and reflexivity in qualitative research. *Qualitative Research, 15*(2), 219–234. https://doi.org/10.1177/1468794112468475

Berger, L., Begun, A., & Otto-Salaj, L. (2009). Participant recruitment in intervention research: Scientific integrity and cost-effective strategies. *International Journal of Social Research Methodology, 12*(1), 79–92. https://doi.org/10.1080/13645570701606077

Berti, A. E., Bombi, A. S., & Duveen, G. T. (1988). *The child's construction of economics*. Editions de la Maison des Sciences de l'Homme.

Bevan, B., Bell, P., Stevens, R., & Razfar, A. (Eds.). (2013). *LOST opportunities: Learning in out-of-school time*. Springer Netherlands.

Biesta, G. (2009). Good education in an age of measurement: On the need to reconnect with the question of purpose in education. *Educational Assessment,*

Evaluation and Accountability, 21(1), 33–46. https://doi.org/10.1007/S11092-008-9064-9

BIS (Department for Business Innovation & Skills). (2012). *The 2011 skills for life survey: A survey of literacy, numeracy and ICT levels in England.* BIS Research Paper Number 81. Crown Copyright.

Blix, S., & Wettergren, Å. (2015). The emotional labour of gaining and maintaining access to the field. *Qualitative Research, 15*(6), 688–704. https://doi.org/10.1177/1468794114561348

Bogotch, I., Mirón, L., & Biesta, G. (2007). "Effective for what; effective for whom?" Two questions SESI should not ignore. In *International handbook of school effectiveness and improvement* (pp. 93–110). Springer.

Bossio, D., Loch, B., Schier, M., & Mazzolini, A. (2014). A roadmap for forming successful interdisciplinary education research collaborations: A reflective approach. *Higher Education Research and Development, 33*(2), 198–211. https://doi.org/10.1080/07294360.2013.832167

Bourke, R., & Loveridge, J. (2014). Exploring informed consent and dissent through children's participation in educational research. *International Journal of Research and Method in Education, 37*(2), 151–165. https://doi.org/10.1080/1743727X.2013.817551

Bradbury, A. (2019). Datafied at four: The role of data in the 'schoolification' of early childhood education in England. *Learning, Media and Technology, 44*(1), 7–21. https://doi.org/10.1080/17439884.2018.1511577

Bradley, J. L., & Conway, P. F. (2016). A dual step transfer model: Sport and non-sport extracurricular activities and the enhancement of academic achievement. *British Educational Research Journal, 42*(4), 703–728. https://doi.org/10.1002/berj.3232

Bronfenbrenner, U. (1986). Ecology of the family as a context for human development: Research perspectives. *Developmental Psychology, 22,* 723–742. https://doi.org/10.1037/0012-1649.22.6.723

Brown, N. (2022). Scope and continuum of participatory research. *International Journal of Research and Method in Education, 45*(2), 200–211. https://doi.org/10.1080/1743727X.2021.1902980

Brown, A. L., & Campione, J. C. (1996). Psychological learning theory and the design of innovative environments: On procedures, principles, and systems. In L. Schauble & R. Glaser (Eds.), *Innovations in learning: New environments for education* (pp. 289–325). Erlbaum.

Brownlie, J. (2019). Out of the ordinary: Research participants' experience of sharing the 'insignificant'. *International Journal of Social Research Methodology, 22*(3), 257–269. https://doi-org.bris.idm.oclc.org/10.1080/13645579.2018.1535880

Carraher, T. N., Carraher, D. W., & Schliemann, A. D. (1985). Mathematics in the streets and in schools. *British Journal of Developmental Psychology, 3*(1), 21–29. https://doi.org/10.1111/j.2044-835X.1985.tb00951.x

Chanfreau, J., Tanner, E., Callanan, M., Laing, K., Skipp, A., & Todd, L. (2016). *Out of school activities during primary school and KS2 attainment.* Centre for Longitudinal Studies Working Paper Series. UCL Institute of Education. https://eprints.ncl.ac.uk/file_store/production/218418/42354AD4-8363-48F0-BFA1-1358B69AA7A0.pdf

Chavkin, N. F. (Ed.). (1993). *Families and schools in a pluralistic society*. State University of New York Press.

Civil, M. (2002). Chapter 4: Everyday mathematics, mathematicians' mathematics, and school mathematics: Can we bring them together? *Journal for Research in Mathematics Education*, 40–62. Monograph, 2002, Vol. 11, Everyday and Academic Mathematics in the Classroom.

Clark, J., & Laing, K. (2022). Case study 5 – Research co-production with young women through an out-of-school residential trip. In J. Rose, T. Jay, J. Goodall, L. Mazzoli Smith, & L. Todd (Eds.), *Repositioning Out-of-School Learning: Methodological challenges and possibilities for researching learning beyond school* (pp. 61–71). Emerald Publishing Limited.

Clark, J., Laing, K., Leat, D., Lofthouse, R., Thomas, U., Tiplady, L., & Woolner, P. (2017). Transformation in interdisciplinary research methodology: The importance of shared experiences in landscapes of practice. *International Journal of Research and Method in Education*, *40*(3), 243–256. https://doi.org/10.1080/174372 7X.2017.1281902

Coles, A., & Scott, H. (2015). Planning for the unexpected in the mathematics classroom: Teacher and student change. *Research in Mathematics Education*, *17*(2), 121–138. https://doi.org/10.1080/14794802.2015.1047787

Collins, C., & Cooper, J. (2014). Emotional intelligence and the qualitative researcher. *International Journal of Qualitative Methods*, *13*(1), 88–103. https://doi.org/ 10.1177/160940691401300134

Cook, D. T. (2001). Exchange value as pedagogy in children's leisure: Moral panics in children's culture at century's end. *Leisure Sciences: An Interdisciplinary Journal*, *23*(2), 81–98. https://doi.org/10.1080/014904001300181684

Coolican, H. (2018). *Research methods and statistics in psychology* (7th ed.). Routledge.

Costas Batlle, I., Mazoli Smith, L., & Cheung Judge, R. (2022). Theme 7 – Slow down: Relationship building and slow research in settings for non-formal learning. In J. Rose, T. Jay, J. Goodall, L. Mazzoli Smith, & L. Todd (Eds.), *Repositioning Out-of-School Learning: Methodological challenges and possibilities for researching learning beyond school* (pp. 169–175). Emerald Publishing Limited.

Crozier, G. (1999). Is it a Case of 'We know when we're not wanted?' The parents' perspective on parent–teacher roles and relationships. *Educational Research*, *41*(3), 315–328. https://doi.org/10.1080/0013188990410306

Crozier, G. (2001). Excluded parents: The deracialisation of parental involvement. *Race, Ethnicity and Education*, *4*(4), 329–341. https://doi.org/10.1080/136133 20120096643

Crozier, G., & Davies, J. (2007). Hard to reach parents or hard to reach schools? A discussion of home-school relations, with particular reference to Bangladeshi and Pakistani parents. *British Educational Research Journal*, *33*(3), 295–313. https:// doi.org/10.1080/01411920701243578

Crozier, G., Reay, D., James, D., Jamieson, F., Beedell, P., Hollingworth, S., & Williams, K. (2008). White middle-class parents, identities, educational choice and the urban comprehensive school: Dilemmas, ambivalence and moral ambiguity. *British Journal of Sociology of Education*, *29*(3), 261–272. https://doi.org/10.1080/ 01425690801966295

Dalby, D., & Noyes, A. (2022). Mathematics curriculum *waves* within vocational education. *Oxford Review of Education, 48*(2), 166–183. https://doi.org/10.1080/03054985.2021.1940913

De Abreu, G., & Cline, T. (2005). Parents' representations of their children's mathematics learning in multiethnic primary schools. *British Educational Research Journal, 31*(6), 697–722. https://doi.org/10.1080/01411920500314869

DePalma, R. (2010). Socially just research for social justice: Negotiating consent and safety in a participatory action research project. *International Journal of Research and Method in Education, 33*(3), 215–227. https://doi.org/10.1080/174372 7X.2010.511713

Department for Business, Innovation and Skills. (2011). *Skills for life survey: Headline findings*. BIS.

Department for Children, Schools, and Families (DCSF). (2008). *The impact of parental involvement on children's education*. DCSF Publications.

Department for Education. (2013). *Mathematics programmes of study: Key stages 1 and 2. National curriculum in England*. Crown Copyright.

Department for Education. (2014a). *National curriculum in England: Mathematics programmes of study*. DfE.

Department of Education. (2014b). [U.S.] Department of Education releases new parent and community engagement framework [blog post]. https://blog.ed.gov/2014/04/department-of-education-releases-new-parent-and-community-engagement-framework/

Department for Education (DfE). (2010). *The importance of teaching: Schools white paper*. Author.

Desforges, C., & Abouchaar, A. (2003). *The impact of parental involvement, parental support and family education on pupil achievement and adjustment: A review of literature*. DfES Publications.

Design-Based Research Collective. (2003). Design-based research: An emerging paradigm for educational inquiry. *Educational Researcher, 32*(1), 5–8. https://doi.org/10.3102/0013189X03200100

Dhillon, J., & Thomas, N. (2019). Ethics of engagement and insider-outsider perspectives: Issues and dilemmas in cross-cultural interpretation. *International Journal of Research and Method in Education, 42*(4), 442–453. https://doi.org/10.1080/1743727X.2018.1533939

Edwards, A. (2011). Building common knowledge at the boundaries between professional practices: Relational agency and relational expertise in systems of distributed expertise. *International Journal of Educational Research, 50*, 33–39. https://doi.org/10.1016/j.ijer.2011.04.007

Edwards, R., & Fowler, Z. (2007). Unsettling boundaries in making a space for research. *British Educational Research Journal, 33*(1), 107–123. https://doi.org/10.1080/01920601104565

Edwards, A., & Mackenzie, L. (2005). Steps towards participation: The social support of learning trajectories. *International Journal of Lifelong Learning, 24*(4), 287–302. https://doi.org/10.1080/02601370500169178

Elliott, L., & Bachman, H. (2018). SES disparities in early math abilities: The contributions of parents' math cognitions, practices to support math, and math talk. *Developmental Review, 49*, 1–15. https://doi.org/10.1016/j.dr.2018.08.001

Engeström, Y. (1987). *Learning by expanding*. Orienta-Konsultit.

Epstein, J. L. (1983). Longitudinal effects of family-school-person interactions on student outcomes. *Research in Sociology of Education and Socialization, 4,* 101–127.

Epstein, J. L. (1991). Effects on student achievement of teachers' practices of parent involvement. In S. B. Silvern (Ed.), *Advances in reading/language research: Vol. 5. Literacy through family, community, and school interaction* (pp. 261–276). JAI Press.

Fan, W., & Williams, C. M. (2009). The effects of parental involvement on students' academic self-efficacy, engagement and intrinsic motivation. *Educational Psychology, 30*(1), 53–74. https://doi.org/10.1080/01443410903353302

Fan, H., Xu, J., Cai, Z., He, J., & Fan, X. (2017). Homework and students' achievement in math and science: A 30-year meta-analysis, 1986–2015. *Educational Research Review, 20,* 35–54. https://doi.org/10.1016/j.edurev.2016.11.003

Feiler, A. (2009). *Engaging 'Hard to Reach' Parents: Teacher-parent collaboration to promote children's learning.* Wiley.

Felton-Koestler, M. (2017). Mathematics education as sociopolitical: Prospective teachers' views of the What, Who, and How. *Journal of Mathematics Teacher Education, 20,* 49–74. https://doi.org/10.1007/s10857-015-9315-x

Fisher, K., McCulloch, A. & Gershuny, J. (1999). *British fathers and children: A report for Channel 4 "Dispatches", Technical report.* Institute for Social and Economic Research.

Fitzmaurice, H., Flynn, M., & Hanafin, J. (2021). Parental involvement in homework: A qualitative Bourdieusian study of class, privilege, and social reproduction. *International Studies in Sociology of Education, 30*(4), 440–461. https://doi.org/10.1080/09620214.2020.1789490

Flewitt, R., Jones, P., Potter, J., Domingo, M., Collins, P., Munday, E., & Stenning, K. (2018). 'I enjoyed it because … you could do whatever you wanted and be creative': Three principles for participatory research and pedagogy. *International Journal of Research and Method in Education, 41*(4), 372–386. https://doi.org/10.1080/1743727X.2017.1405928

Flouri, E., & Buchanan, A. (2004). Early father's and mother's involvement and child's later educational outcomes. *British Journal of Educational Psychology, 74,* 141–153. https://doi.org/10.1348/000709904773839806

Floyd, A., & Arthur, L. (2012). Researching from within: External and internal ethical engagement. *International Journal of Research and Method in Education, 35*(2), 171–180. https://doi.org/10.1080/1743727X.201.670481

Frankenstein, M. (2009). Developing a critical mathematical numeracy through *real* real-life word problems. In L. Verschaffel, B. Greer, W. Van Dooran, & S. Mukhopadhyay (Eds.), *Words and Worlds: Modeling verbal descriptions of situations* (pp. 111–130). Sense Publishers.

Furnham, A. (2001). Parental attitudes to pocket money/allowances for children. *Journal of Economic Psychology, 22*(3), 397–422. https://doi.org/10.1016/S0167-4870(01)00040-X

Garg, R., Kauppi, C., Lewko, J., & Urajnik, D. (2002). A structural model of educational aspirations. *Journal of Career Development, 29,* 87–108. https://doi.org/10.1023/A:1019964119690

Gauthier, A. H., Smeeding, T. M., & Furstenberg, F. F. (2004). Are parents investing less time in children? Trends in selected industrialized countries. *Population and*

Development Review, 30(4), 647–672. https://doi.org/10.1111/j.1728-4457. 2004.00036.x

Ginsburg, A., & Smith, M. (2016). *Do randomised controlled trials meet the gold standard?* American Enterprise Institute. http://www.aei.org/wp-content/uploads/2016/03/Dorandomized-controlled-trials-meet-the-gold-standard.pdf

Goff, W. (2020). Gatekeeper engagement and the importance of phronesis-praxis in school-based research. *New Zealand Journal of Educational Studies, 55*, 321–335. https://doi.org/10.1007/s40841-020-00177-x

Goldman, S., & Booker, A. (2009). Making math a definition of the situation: Families as sites for mathematical practices. *Anthropology & Education Quarterly, 40*(4), 369–387. https://doi.org/10.1111/j.1548-1492.2009.01057.x

González, N., Moll, L. C., & Amanti, C. (Eds.). (2005). *Funds of knowledge: Theorizing practices in households, communities, and classrooms.* Lawrence Erlbaum Associates Publishers.

González, N., Moll, L. C., & Amanti, C. (Eds.). (2006). *Funds of knowledge: Theorizing practices in households, communities, and classrooms.* Routledge.

Goodall, J. (2017). *Narrowing the achievement gap: Parental engagement with children's learning.* Routledge.

Goodall, J. (2022). Concluding thoughts. In J. Rose, T. Jay, J. Goodall, L. Mazzoli Smith, & L. Todd (Eds.), *Repositioning Out-of-School Learning: Methodological challenges and possibilities for researching learning beyond school* (pp. 177–184). Emerald Publishing Limited.

Goodall, J., & Montgomery, C. (2014). Parental involvement to parental engagement: A continuum. *Educational Review, 66*(4), 399–410. https://doi.org/10.1080/00131911.2013.781576

Goodall, J., & Vorhaus, J. (2011). *Review of best practice in parental engagement.* Department of Education.

Gorard, S., & Huat See, B. (2013). *Do parental involvement interventions increase attainment? A review of the evidence.* Nuffield Foundation. https://www.nuffieldfoundation.org/sites/default/files/files/Do_parental_involvement_interventions_increase_attainment1.pdf

Greeno, J. G. (1997). On claims that answer the wrong questions. *Educational Researcher, 26*(1), 5–17. https://doi.org/10.3102/0013189X026001005

Greer, B., & Mukhopadhyay, S. (2003). What is mathematics education for? *Mathematics Educator, 13*(2), 2–6.

Gristy, C. (2015). Engaging with and moving on from participatory research: A personal reflection. *International Journal of Research and Method in Education, 38*(4), 371–387. https://doi.org/10.1080/1743727X.2014.940306

Guberman, S. R. (2004). A comparative study of children's out-of-school activities and arithmetical achievements. *Journal for Research in Mathematics Education, 35*(2), 117–150. https://doi.org/10.2307/30034934

Guillemin, M., Barnard, E., Allen, A., Stewart, P., Walker, H., Rosenthal, D., & Gillam, L. (2018). Do research participants trust researchers or their institution? *Journal of Empirical Research on Human Research Ethics: An International Journal, 13*(3), 285–294. https://doi.org/10.1177/1556264618763

Gunderson, E. A., Ramirez, G., Levine, S. C., & Beilock, S. L. (2012). The role of parents and teachers in the development of gender-related math attitudes. *Sex Roles, 66*(3), 153–166. https://doi.org/10.1007/s11199-011-9996-2

Gutstein, E. (2006). *Reading and writing the world with mathematics: Toward a pedagogy for social justice.* Routledge.

Haines Lyon, C. (2022). Case study 8 – Destabilising methodologies: Working towards democratic parent engagement. In J. Rose, T. Jay, J. Goodall, L. Mazzoli Smith, & L. Todd (Eds.), *Repositioning Out-of-School Learning: Methodological challenges and possibilities for researching learning beyond school* (pp. 97–107). Emerald Publishing Limited.

Harris, A., & Goodall, J. (2008). Do parents know they matter? Engaging all parents in learning. *Educational Research, 50*(3), 277–289. https://doi.org/10.1080/00131880802309424

Hayward, G., & Fernandez, R. (2004). From core skills to key skills: Fast forward or back to the future? *Oxford Review of Education, 30*(1), 117–145. https://doi.org/10.1080/0305498042000190087

Hedges, H. (2010). Blurring the boundaries: Connecting research, practice and professional learning. *Cambridge Journal of Education, 40*(3), 299–314. https://doi.org/10.1080/0305764X.2010.502884

Heffner, A., & Antaramian, S. (2016). The role of life satisfaction in predicting student engagement and achievement. *Journal of Happiness Studies, 17*, 1681–1701. https://doi.org/10.1007/s10902-015-9665-1

Hoover-Dempsey, K. V., Walker, J. M. T., Sandler, H. M., Whetsel, D., Green, C. L., Wilkins, A. S., & Closson, K. (2005). Why do parents become involved? Research findings and implications. *The Elementary School Journal, 106*(2), 105–130. https://doi.org/10.1086/499194

Hornby, G., & Blackwell, I. (2018). Barriers to parental involvement in education: An update. *Educational Review, 70*(1), 109–119. https://doi.org/10.1080/00131911.2018.1388612

Hornby, G., & Lafaele, R. (2011). Barriers to parental involvement in education: An explanatory model. *Educational Review, 63*(1), 37–52. https://doi.org/10.1080/00131911.2010.488049

Ho Sui-Chu, El., & Williams, J. D. (1996). Effects of parental involvement on 8th grade achievement. *Sociology of Education, 69*(2), 126–141. https://doi.org/10.2307/2112802

Huat See, B., & Gorard, S. (2015). Does intervening to enhance parental involvement in education lead to better academic results for children? An extended review. *Journal of Children's Services, 10*(3), 252–264. https://doi.org/10.1108/JCS-02-2015-0008

Hughes, R. (1998). Why do people agree to participate in social research? The case of drug injectors. *International Journal of Social Research Methodology, 1*(4), 315–324. https://doi.org/10.1080/13645579.1998.10846883

Hughes, M., & Greenhough, P. (2011). Knowledge exchange activities for home-school communication. In K. Safford, M. Stacey, & R. Hancock (Eds.), *Small-scale research in primary schools: A reader for learning and professional development.* Routledge. https://doi.org/10.4324/9781315881225

Hughes, M., & Pollard, A. (2006). Home–school knowledge exchange in context. *Educational Review, 58*(4), 385–395. https://doi.org/10.1080/00131910600971784

Israel, B., Schulz, A., Parker, E., Becker, A., Allen, A., Guzman, J., & Lichtenstein, R. (2017). Critical issues in developing and following CBPR Principles. In N. Wallerstein, B. Duran, J. Oetzel, & M. Minkler (Eds.), *Community-based participatory research for health: Advancing social and health equity* (3rd ed., pp. 31–43). Wiley.

Jay, T., & Laing, K. (2022). Theme 1 – Negotiating the researcher role in out-of-school learning research. In J. Rose, T. Jay, J. Goodall, L. Mazzoli Smith, & L. Todd (Eds.), *Repositioning Out-of-School Learning: Methodological challenges and possibilities for researching learning beyond school* (pp. 123–129). Emerald Publishing Limited.

Jay, T., & Rose, J. (2022). Case study 3 – Researching the unknown: Developing an understanding of children's informal mathematical activity. In J. Rose, T. Jay, J. Goodall, L. Mazzoli Smith, & L. Todd (Eds.,) *Repositioning out-of-school learning: Methodological challenges and possibilities for researching learning beyond school* (pp. 39–48). Emerald Publishers.

Jay, T., Rose, J., & Simmons, B. (2017). Finding 'mathematics': Parents questioning school-centred approaches to involvement in children's mathematics learning. *School Community Journal, 27*(1), 201–230. https://www.schoolcommunity network.org/SCJ.aspx

Jay, T., Rose, J., & Simmons, B. (2018). Why is parental involvement in children's mathematics learning hard? Parental perspectives on their role supporting children's learning. *Sage Open,* 1–13. https://doi.org/10.1177/2158244018775466

Jeynes, W. (2012). A meta-analysis of the efficacy of different types of parental involvement programs for urban students. *Urban Education, 47*(4), 706–742. https://doi.org/10.1177/0042085912445643

Jones, L., & Allebone, B. (1999). Researching 'hard-to-reach' groups: The crucial role of the research associate. *International Journal of Inclusive Education, 3*(4), 353–362. https://doi.org/10.1080/136031199284986

Keil, F. (1986). Conceptual domains and the acquisition of metaphor. *Cognitive Development, 1*(1), 73–96. https://doi.org/10.1016/S0885-2014(86)80024-7

Keiner, E. (2019). 'Rigour', 'discipline' and the 'systematic': The cultural construction of educational research identities? *European Educational Research Journal, 18*(5), 527–545. https://doi.org/10.1177/1474904118824935

Kuckzera, M., Field, S., & Windisch, H. C. (2016). *Building skills for all: A review of England.* OECD.

Leiser, D., & Beth Halachmi, R. (2006). Children's understanding of market forces. *Journal of Economic Psychology, 27*(1), 6–19. https://doi.org/10.1016/j.joep.2005. 06.008

Levine, S. C., Suriyakham, L. W., Rowe, M. L., Huttenlocher, J., & Gunderson, E. A. (2010). What counts in the development of young children's number knowledge? *Developmental Psychology, 46*(5), 1309–1319. https://doi.org/10.1037/a0019671

Lewis, R. (2009). Recruiting parents and children into a research project: A qualitative exploration of families' decision-making processes. *International Journal of Social Research Methodology, 12*(5), 405–419. https://doi.org/10.1080/1364557 0802289104

Lutz, A., & Jayaram, L. (2015). Getting the homework done: Social class and parents' relationship to homework. *International Journal of Education and Social Science, 2*(6), 73–84.

Ma, X. (2001). Participation in advanced mathematics: Do expectation and influence of students, peers, teachers, and parents matter? *Contemporary Educational Psychology, 26*(1), 132–146. https://doi.org/10.1006/ceps.2000.1050

Mader, C., Scott, G., & Razak, D. A. (2013). Effective change management, governance and policy for sustainability transformation in higher education. *Sustainability Accounting, Management and Policy Journal, 4*(3), 264–284. https://doi.org/10.1108/SAMPJ-09-2013-0037

Maloney, E. A., Ramirez, G., Gunderson, E. A., Levine, S. C., & Beilock, S. L. (2015). Intergenerational effects of parents' math anxiety on children's math achievement and anxiety. *Psychological Science, 26*(9), 1480–1488. https://doi.org/10.1177/0956797615592630

Mapp, K. L., & Kuttner, P. J. (2013). *Partners in education: A dual capacity-building framework for family–school partnerships.* SEDL. http://www2.ed.gov/documents/family-community/partners-education.pdf

Mau, W. C. (1997). Parental influences on the high school students' academic achievement: A comparison of Asian immigrants, Asian Americans, and White Americans. *Psychology in the Schools, 34*(3), 267–277. https://doi.org/10.1002/(SICI)1520-6807(199707)34:3%3C267::AID-PITS9%3E3.0.CO;2-L

McCowan, T. (2018). Five perils of the impact agenda in higher education. *London Review of Education, 16*(2), 279–295. https://doi.org/10.18546/LRE.16.2.08

McGarry, O. (2016). Repositioning the research encounter: Exploring power dynamics and positionality in youth research. *International Journal of Social Research Methodology, 19*(3), 339–354. https://doi.org/10.1080/13645579.2015.1011821

McMullen, R., & de Abreu, G. (2011). Mothers' experiences of their children's school mathematics at home: The impact of being a mother-teacher. *Research in Mathematics Education, 13*(1), 59–74. https://doi.org/10.1080/14794802.2011.550727

McNamara, A., Akiva, T., & Delale-O'Connor, L. (2020). Opportunity gaps in out-of-school learning: How structural and process features of programs relate to race and socioeconomic status. *Applied Developmental Science, 24*(4), 360–375. https://doi.org/10.1080/10888691.2018.1513794

McNeal, R. (2001). Differential effects of parental involvement on cognitive and behavioral outcomes by socioeconomic status. *The Journal of Socio-Economics, 30*(2), 171–179. https://doi.org/10.1016/S1053-5357(00)00100-1

Mearns, T., Coyle, D., & de Graaff, R. (2014). Aspirations and assumptions: A researcher's account of pupil involvement in school-based research. *International Journal of Research and Method in Education, 37*(4), 442–457. https://doi.org/10.1080/1743727X.2014.952440

Melhuish, E., Phan, M., Sylva, K., Sammons, P., Siraj-Blatchford, I., & Taggart, B. (2008). Effects of the home learning environment and preschool center experience upon literacy and numeracy development in early primary school. *Journal of Social Issues, 64*(1), 95–114. https://doi.org/10.1111/j.1540-4560.2008.00550.x

Metzger, S. R., Sonnenschein, S., & Galindo, C. (2019). Elementary-age children's conceptions about mathematics utility and their home-based mathematics engagement. *The Journal of Educational Research, 112*(4), 431–446. https://doi.org/10.1080/00220671.2018.1547961

Milligan, L. (2016). Insider-outsider-inbetweener? Researcher positioning, participative methods and cross-cultural educational research. *Compare: A Journal of Comparative and International Education, 46*(2), 235–250. https://doi.org/10.1080/03057925.2014.928510

Mills, J. (2012). *Key statistics about Bristol from the 2011 census.* Bristol City Council. https://www.bristol.gov.uk/documents/20182/34008/2011%20Census%20Key%20Statistics%20about%20Bristol%20LA%20areaUpdate.pdf. Accessed on June 22, 2018.

Mills, J. (2015). *Deprivation in Bristol 2015: The mapping of deprivation within Bristol local authority area.* Bristol City Council. https://www.bristol.gov.uk/documents/20182/32951/Deprivation+in+Bristol+2015/429b2004-eeff-44c5-8044-9e7dcd002faf. Accessed on June 22, 2018.

Moll, L., Amanti, C., Neff, D., & Gonzalez, N. (1992). Funds of knowledge for teaching: Using a qualitative approach to connect homes and classrooms. *Theory Into Practice, 31*(2), 132–141. https://doi.org/10.1080/00405849209543534

Moss, P. (2008). What future for the relationship between early childhood education and care and compulsory schooling? *Research in Comparative and International Education, 3*(3), 224–234. https://doi.org/10.2304/rcie.2008.3.3.224

Moss, P. (2013). *Early childhood and compulsory education: Reconceptualising the relationship.* Routledge.

Mullis, I. V., Martin, M. O., Foy, P., & Arora, A. (2012). *TIMSS 2011 international results in mathematics.* International Association for the Evaluation of Educational Achievement.

Nairn, K., Showden, C., Sligo, J., Matthews, K., & Kidman, J. (2020). Consent requires a relationship: Rethinking group consent and its timing in ethnographic research. *International Journal of Social Research Methodology, 23*(6), 719–731. https://doi.org/10.1080/13645579.2020.1760562

National Institute of Adult Continuing Education. (2011). *Numeracy counts: NIACE committee of inquiry on adult numeracy learning (final report).* NIACE.

Netolicky, D., & Barnes, N. (2018). Method as a journey: A narrative dialogic partnership illuminating decision-making in qualitative educational research. *International Journal of Research and Method in Education, 41*(5), 500–513. https://doi.org/10.1080/1743727X.2017.1295938

Nukaga, M. (2008). The underlife of kids' school lunchtime. *Journal of Contemporary Ethnography, 37*(3), 342.

Oates, T. (2011). Could do better: Using international comparisons to refine the National Curriculum in England. *Curriculum Journal, 22*(2), 121–150. https://doi.org/10.1080/09585176.2011.578908

Ofsted. (2017). *Bold beginnings: The Reception curriculum in a sample of good and outstanding primary schools.* Crown Copyright.

Oikonomidoy, E., & Wiest, L. (2017). Navigating cross-boundary connections in educational research. *International Journal of Research and Method in Education, 40*(1), 53–65. https://doi.org/10.1080/1743727X.2015.1036851

Österman, T., & Bråting, K. (2019). Dewey and mathematical practice: Revisiting the distinction between procedural and conceptual knowledge. *Journal of Curriculum Studies, 51*(4), 457–470. https://doi.org/10.1080/00220272.2019.1594388

Otto, A., Schots, P. A. M., Westerman, J. A. J., & Webley, P. (2006). Children's use of saving strategies: An experimental approach. *Journal of Economic Psychology, 27*(1), 57–72. https://doi.org/10.1016/j.joep.2005.06.013

Parker, A., & Tritter, J. (2006). Focus group method and methodology: Current practice and recent debate. *International Journal of Research and Method in Education, 29*(1), 23–37. https://doi.org/10.1080/01406720500537304

Patall, E. A., Cooper, H., & Robinson, J. C. (2008). Parent involvement in homework: A research synthesis. *Review of Educational Research, 78*(4), 1039–1101. https://doi.org/10.3102/0034654308325185

Pekrun, R., Goetz, T., Titz, W., & Perry, R. (2002). Academic emotions in students' self-regulated learning and achievement: A program of qualitative and quantitative research. *Educational Psychologist, 37*(2), 91–105. https://doi.org/10.1207/S15326985EP3702_4

Peters, M., Seeds, K., Goldstein, A., & Coleman, N. (2008). *Parental involvement in children's education 2007 (Research Report DCSF-RR034).* Department for Children, Schools and Families.

Pilcher, K., Martin, W., & Williams, V. (2016). Issues of collaboration, representation, meaning and emotions: Utilising participant-led visual diaries to capture the everyday lives of people in mid to later life. *International Journal of Social Research Methodology, 19*(6), 677–692. https://doi.org/10.1080/13645579.2017.1287875

Pole, C., Mien, P., & Bolton, A. (1999). Realising children's agency in research: Partners and participants? *International Journal of Social Research Methodology, 2*(1), 39–54. https://doi.org/10.1080/1364557995177

Popovic, G., & Lederman, J. (2015). Implications of informal education experiences for mathematics teachers' ability to make connections beyond formal classroom. *School Science & Mathematics, 115*(3), 129–140. https://doi.org/10.1111/ssm.12114

Ratto, A., Anthony, B., Pugliese, C., Mendez, R., Safer-Lichtenstein, J., Dudley, K., Kahn, N., Kenworthy, L., Biel, M., Martucci, J., & Anthony, L. (2017). Lessons learned: Engaging culturally diverse families in neurodevelopmental disorders intervention research. *Autism, 21*(5), 622–634. https://doi.org/10.1177/1362361316650394

Redding, S., Langdon, J., Meyer, J., & Sheley, P. (2004). *The effects of comprehensive parent engagement on student learning outcomes.* Harvard Family Research Project. https://archive.globalfrp.org/publications-resources/browse-our-publications/the-effects-of-comprehensive-parent-engagement-on-student-learning-outcomes

Rönkä, A., Sevõn, E., Malinen, K., & Salonen, E. (2014). An examination of nonresponse in a study on daily family life: I do not have time to participate, but I can tell you something about our life. *International Journal of Social Research Methodology, 17*(3), 197–214. https://doi.org/10.1080/13645579.2012.729401

Rose, J. (2011). Dilemmas of interprofessional collaboration: Can they be resolved? *Children & Society, 25*(2), 151–163. https://doi.org/10.1111/j.1099-0860.2009.00268.x

Rose, J., & Jay, T. (2022). Case study 7 – Reflections on position: Relational agency in researching 'everyday maths'. In J. Rose, T. Jay, J. Goodall, L. Mazzoli Smith, & L. Todd (Eds.), *Repositioning Out-of-School Learning: Methodological challenges and possibilities for researching learning beyond school* (pp. 85–96): Emerald Publishing Limited.

Rose, J., Jay, T., Goodall, J., Mazzoli-Smith, L., & Todd, L. (2022). *Repositioning out-of-school learning: Methodological challenges and possibilities for researching learning beyond school.* Emerald Publishing Limited.

Rose, J., & Todd, L. (2022). Theme 2 – Building relationships, building structure: Working together in research on out-of-school learning. In J. Rose, T. Jay, J. Goodall, L. Mazzoli Smith, & L. Todd (Eds.), *Repositioning Out-of-School*

Learning: Methodological challenges and possibilities for researching learning beyond school (pp. 131–139). Emerald Publishing Limited.

Rossi, P., Freeman, H., & Lipsey, M. (1999). *Evaluation: A systematic approach*. Sage.

Sayer, L. C., Bianchi, S. M., & Robinson, J. P. (2004). Are parents investing less in children? Trends in mothers' and fathers' time with children. *American Journal of Sociology, 110*(1), 1–43. https://doi.org/10.1086/386270

Schlebe, L., Chanmugam, A., Moses, T., Saltzburg, S., Rankin Williams, L., & Letendre, J. (2015). Youth participation in qualitative research: Challenges and possibilities. *Qualitative Social Work, 14*(4), 504–521. https://doi.org/10.1177/1473325014556792

Skwarchuk, S. L., Sowinski, C., & LeFevre, J. A. (2014). Formal and informal home learning activities in relation to children's early numeracy and literacy skills: The development of a home numeracy model. *Journal of Experimental Child Psychology, 121*, 63–84. https://doi.org/10.1016/j.jecp.2013.11.006

Stacey, K. (2015). The international assessment of mathematical literacy: PISA 2012 framework and items. In *Selected regular lectures from the 12th International Congress on Mathematical Education* (pp. 771–790): Springer.

Stanley, G. (2006). Seven principles for change management. *Sustainable Leadership in Education*, 1–10.

Star, J. (2005). Reconceptualising procedural knowledge. *Journal for Research in Mathematics Education, 36*(5), 404–411. https://doi.org/10.2307/30034943

Stevens, R. (2013). What counts too much and too little as math. In B. Bevan, P. Bell, R. Stevens, & A. Razfar (Eds.), *Lost opportunities: Learning in out-of-school time* (pp. 65–83). Springer.

Sung, N. S., Crowley, W. F., Jr., Genel, M., et al. (2003). Central challenges facing the national clinical research enterprise. *JAMA, 289*(10), 1278–1287. https://doi.org/10.1001/jama.289.10.1278

Susperreguy, M. I., & Davis-Kean, P. E. (2016). Maternal math talk in the home and math skills in preschool children. *Early Education and Development, 27*(6), 841–857. https://doi.org/10.1080/10409289.2016.1148480

Taylor, E. V. (2009). The purchasing practice of low-income students: The relationship to mathematical development. *The Journal of the Learning Sciences, 18*(3), 370–415. https://doi.org/10.1080/10508400903013462

Thomson, R., & Holland, J. (2003). Hindsight, foresight and insight: The challenges of longitudinal qualitative research. *International Journal of Social Research Methodology, 6*(3), 233–244. https://doi.org/10.1080/1364557032000091833

Tracy, S. (2010). Qualitative quality: Eight "big-tent" criteria for excellent qualitative research. *Qualitative Inquiry, 16*, 837–851. https://doi.org/10.1177/1077800410383121

Turner, E., Varley Gutiérrez, M., Simic-Muller, K., & Díez-Palomar, J. (2009). "Everything is math in the whole world": Integrating critical and community knowledge in authentic mathematical investigations with elementary latina/o students. *Mathematical Thinking and Learning, 11*(3), 136–157. https://doi.org/10.1080/10986060903013382

Webley, P. (1996). Playing the market: The autonomous economic world of children. In P. K. Lunt & A. Furnham (Eds.), *Economic socialization. The economic beliefs and behaviours of young people* (pp. 149–161). Edward Elgar Publishing Limited.

Webley, P., & Lea, S. E. (1993). Towards a more realistic psychology of economic socialization. *Journal of Economic Psychology*, *14*(3), 461–472. https://doi.org/10.1016/0167-4870(93)90027-I

Wenger, E. (1998). *Communities of practice: Learning, meaning, and identity*. Cambridge University Press.

Williams, J., & Choudry, S. (2016). Mathematics capital in the educational field: Bourdieu and beyond. *Research in Mathematics Education*, *18*(1), 3–21. https://doi.org/10.1080/14794802.2016.1141113

Williams, P. (2008). *Independent Review of Mathematics Teaching in Early Years Settings and Primary Education*. Department for Children, Schools and Families.

Wilson, S. (2020). 'Hard to reach' parents but not hard to research: A critical reflection of gatekeeper positionality using a community-based methodology. *International Journal of Research and Method in Education*, *44*(5), 461–477. https://doi.org/10.1080/1743727X.2019.1626819

Wilson, E., Kenny, A., & Dickson-Swift, V. (2018). Ethical challenges of community based participatory research: Exploring researchers' experience. *International Journal of Social Research Methodology*, *21*(1), 7–24. https://doi.org/10.1080/13645579.2017.1296714

Winter, J., Salway, L., Yee, W. C., & Hughes, M. (2004). Linking home and school mathematics: The home school knowledge exchange project. *Research in Mathematics Education*, *6*(1), 59–75. https://doi.org/10.1080/14794800008520130

Woolf, S. H. (2008). The meaning of translational research and why it matters. *JAMA*, *299*(2), 211–213. https://doi.org/10.1001/jama.2007.26

Woolf, S. H., Purnell, J. Q., Simon, S. M., Zimmerman, E. B., Camberos, G. J., Haley, A., & Fields, R. P. (2015). Translating evidence into population health improvement: Strategies and barriers. *Annual Review of Public Health*, *36*, 463–482. https://doi.org/10.1146/annurev-publhealth-082214-110901

Xolocotzin, U., & Jay, T. (2020). Children's perspectives on their economic activity – Diversity, motivations and parental awareness. *Children & Society*, *34*(5), 424–442. https://doi.org/10.1111/chso.12377

Index

Printed and bound by CPI Group (UK) Ltd, Croydon, CR0 4YY

04/01/2024

08217062-0004